WITHDRAWN

In Flanders fields the poppies blow
Between the crosses, row on row,
  That mark our place; and in the sky
  The larks, still bravely singing, fly
Scarce heard amid the guns below.

We are the Dead. Short days ago
We lived, felt dawn, saw sunset glow,
  Loved, and were loved, and now we lie
    In Flanders fields.

Take up our quarrel with the foe:
To you from failing hands we throw
  The torch; be yours to hold it high.
  If ye break faith with us who die
We shall not sleep, though poppies grow
    In Flanders fields.

Flanders fields the poppies
een the crosses, row on row
mark our place: and in
larks still bravely singing,
ce heard amid the guns b

or the Dead. Short days a
lived, felt dawn, saw sunse
d, and were loved, and now
Flanders fields.

up our quarrel with the fo
m from failing hands we th
torch: be yours to hold it h
e break faith with us who d
shall not sleep, though poppi
Flanders fields.

IN FLANDERS FIELDS

100 YEARS

EDITED BY AMANDA BETTS

Alfred A. Knopf Canada

Case *(front and back):*
Soldiers' Tower Memorial
Screen, University of Toronto

Endpaper *(front):*
David Milne, "Courcelette from
the Cemetery, July, 1919."

Page i:
Passchendaele, Belgium,
November 1917.

Page ii:
Valley of the Somme, France.

Page iii:
Lijssenthoek Military Cemetery,
Belgium, circa 1918.

Page iv:
Members of No. 1 Platoon,
3rd Divisional Cyclist Company,
Canadian Army, 1915.

Page v:
Westminster Abbey,
London, 2014.

Page vi:
Detail of "In Flanders Fields," in
McCrae's original handwriting.

Page x:
Canadian officer's hand-drawn
strategic map, 1917.

Page xi:
Cratered remains, Lens, France,
February 1918.

Page x:
Morning mist, Flanders, Belgium.

PUBLISHED BY ALFRED A. KNOPF CANADA

Pages 253 to 257 constitute a continuation of the
copyright page.

www.penguinrandomhouse.ca

LIBRARY AND ARCHIVES CANADA
CATALOGUING IN PUBLICATION

In Flanders Fields : 100 years : writing on war, loss and
remembrance / Amanda Betts, editor.

Essays and poems.
Issued in print and electronic formats.

ISBN 978-0-345-81025-0
eBook ISBN 978-0-345-81027-4

1. McCrae, John, 1872–1918. In Flanders fields. 2. World
War, 1914–1918—Canada—Literature and the war.
3. World War, 1914–1918—Influence. 4. Collective
memory—Canada. 5. Collective memory and
literature—Canada. 6. Remembrance Day (Canada).
7. World War, 1914–1918—Canada. I. Betts, Amanda,
editor

PS8525.C73Z6 2015   C811'.52   C2015-902685-7

Jacket image: © Nella | Shutterstock.com

Printed and bound in Canada

10 9 8 7 6 5 4 3 2 1

Penguin
Random House
KNOPF CANADA

CONTENTS

In Flanders Fields

"EARLSCOURT"
THESE FOUR MOTHERS
GAVE TO THEIR COUNTRY
28 BRAVE SONS

ROMÉO DALLAIRE
THOSE WHO SERVE

A COPY OF "IN FLANDERS FIELDS," in John McCrae's own hand, hung above my desk in the Senate. When I first read it, as a boy in the 1950s—decades after it had been written—war had been a part of everyday life for generations. After two world wars, concepts like patriotism and unity against a common enemy felt absolute, and McCrae's poem was like a torch being passed to every child, woman and man, evoking a communal understanding of the importance of sacrifice.

Today, we no longer enjoy this unity of understanding. Our country is at a restless peace, while the world is rife with conflicts that are complex, messy, unpredictable and borderless. Belligerents are playing by a new set of rules, and we still haven't seen the playbook. Yet "In Flanders Fields" is far from being irrelevant in this new world disorder. Its timeless meaning endures, though McCrae's words speak more personally now.

The power of this poem, which has survived the hundred years of war and peace since it was written, now lies in its many resonances—perhaps as many as it has readers.

WHEN MOST CANADIANS today read or hear those familiar words, on Remembrance Day perhaps, they commemorate the end of "the war to end war," and the too-many wars waged

Warriors Day Parade, Toronto, 1920.

since. "In Flanders Fields" sparks two minutes of respectful silence for the Dead, who lived, loved, and were loved. For two minutes each year, many pause to remember. Some even shed tears. But then, inevitably, many forget.

At the time the poem was published, however, Canada—and the world—was at war. There wasn't a single person not profoundly affected and intimately involved—from a logger on the Queen Charlotte Islands to a suffragette in Winnipeg, from the son of an oil refiner in East Montreal to a fisherman's daughter in Antigonish—and especially the young men who enthusiastically joined the fight, supported by their families, their hometowns and the country as a whole.

Their patriotism was a given, and the nobility of soldiering went unquestioned. In English Canada, those few who did not support the war effort were shunned (in my home province of Quebec, things were always more complicated, though over a hundred thousand Quebecers fought in the two world wars). Men joined the fighting forces proud and eager, knowing that a bullet or a bayonet might have their name on it. That was all part of the glorious sacrifice.

But the realities of war were much bleaker. While soldiers were trained to expect death, they were not expecting chlorine gas.

In the Second Battle of Ypres (during which "In Flanders Fields" is thought to have been composed), chemical attacks were used for the first time. Instead of a single shot stealing the life from his brothers, McCrae would have witnessed men dying after six to ten hours of terrible agony, turned on their sides, quite literally coughing their lungs out. The German troops who dispersed the gas were so frightened of its effects, they refused to exploit the gap in the front lines that the chemical assault created.

Most soldiers on both sides in this war were trained well

enough that they could calmly weigh their own mortality under assault, except when it came to gas. A telling point: historian Jason Wilson notes that soldiers performing in the various regimental morale-boosting concert parties could tap just about any topic for their trench-side comedy routines: the futility of war, bull-headed officers, conditions on the front line, even death. Everything was fair game, with this one exception: in the minds of these soldiers, there was nothing funny about chlorine gas.

McCrae must have desperately needed to make something of this terrible death inflicted on his brothers-in-arms. Images of poppies—bold yet fragile, ephemeral yet enduring—instead of young men writhing in agony, were fitting for the time: the horrors of war were not talked about outright. They were too painful to recount, and civilians could only fail to understand.

This is still a challenge, when appropriate therapy and peer support can mean the difference between life and death for veterans suffering trauma when they return home. There are some things you just don't talk about: this was true in McCrae's time and, to a certain extent, it remains true to this day. Hence the generations of too many fathers on Legion barstools, drinking to forget.

My father's generation certainly believed no good could come of dwelling on the horrors. They, and McCrae's generation before them, believed that unveiling the realities of war would frighten even the stalwart, discourage enlistment, allow evil to reign. For McCrae, what could be done, through verse, was to encourage all to join the fight and stop the perpetrators of this most barbarous murder.

I try to imagine what my father might have felt on reading "In Flanders Fields." When it came to his own war, he hated the

Remembrance Day rituals, but I hope he was stirred by McCrae's tribute to the fallen and his reminder of the beautiful things in the world that warrant such sacrifice.

To veterans of more recent conflicts and those currently in active service, McCrae's poem is more than just evocative. It can succeed in expatriating us back to our own battlefields. The glow of the sun rising at dawn. The sound of a lark's wing cutting the air. A glimpse of poppy red. These are but a few of the tiny sensory triggers that can bring a soldier back to the battlefield.

When I read "In Flanders Fields," I do not reminisce—I relive. I, like many others, have been in the midst of war and human destruction, and McCrae's words unfurl in each of my senses, awakening in me the smell of death, the sound of children's cries, the taste of gunpowder in the air. I feel the horror and the fear. I witness again the incredible suffering of the innocent.

It doesn't evoke a memory; it evokes a *reality*. I would wager that when veterans of any conflict, as well as those humanitarians and diplomats who are, more and more, caught up in today's complex missions, read McCrae's words, they are transported, as I am, back to those terrifying places where their work, their duty and their service to humanity brought them.

Just as it subtly recalled the First World War gas attacks for the old guard, "In Flanders Fields" reminds modern soldiers of the even more unthinkable techniques and unspeakable horrors they have witnessed in modern conflicts, which follow no rules, defend no borders, offend all moralities.

Until the end of the Cold War, in most cases, our military faced a recognizable enemy, fought a trained and willing soldier, on a set battlefield, over clear principles. And after the Cold War,

A glimpse of red: *The Brooding Soldier* Memorial, St. Julien, Belgium.

THIS·COLUMN·M
BATTLEFIELD·WH
CANADIANS·ON·T
LEFT·WITHSTOOD
GERMAN·GAS·AT
22-24 APRIL 1915·
AND·LIE·BURIE

we continued training for these classic wars. This was certainly the conventional warfare I was prepared for.

What I found in Rwanda was not. Neither was Afghanistan. Neither is Syria nor the Central African Republic. Often called "dirty wars," these are complex conflicts about which we know little and on which we impose outdated understanding and methods at our peril.

We may look to the Islamic State, al Qaeda or Boko Haram (or to the all-encompassing idea of terror) for a common enemy, but the majority of belligerents today are more enigmatic. In most post–Cold War conflicts, there have been no "redcoats," no "no man's land." In Rwanda, there was no set battlefield, no front line—or rather, there was nothing but a front line. In a hundred days, we saw almost a million civilians butchered— babies, mothers, elderly women, old men, young men. The trained soldiers we faced? Often children—boys and girls, delirious from booze and drugs and hate propaganda, wielding crude but lethal weapons. Such is warfare in the twenty-first century: no longer nation states spilling military blood, but innocent civilian populations being bled within their own borders.

I believe that "In Flanders Fields" is still a credo for all of us who wear the uniform as we come to grips with this confusing era into which we've stumbled. No more do we find millions of professional soldiers fighting millions of professional soldiers. We find instead fewer, ill-prepared soldiers, fighting unconventional forces to protect millions of civilians from mass atrocities—their aim being to stabilize imploding nations and failing states from the overt destruction and unimaginable abuse of civil wars. This is an object worth the sacrifice McCrae described so long ago, but one that is so much harder to defend at home.

There was nothing in our training to prepare us for this. Nor is there any universal endorsement of the value of our interventions in these dirty wars. What we face today has not only caught us by surprise but is an assault on the world that makes sense to us. And it renders our resolve to fight, even to the point of the ultimate sacrifice, all the more complicated. The new breed of belligerents plays by no rule of law with which we are familiar, not the law of armed conflict, not humanitarian law. This, of course, makes it easy for the general population to shirk from the idea of war, preferring self-protective ignorance to paying the cost of helping to secure human lives and rights in faraway lands. It is easy for those not in uniform to misunderstand the compulsion that drives soldiers to fight for what is right and good and not just hope and pray for it.

JOHN McCRAE'S DEDICATION to the war effort, his devotion to duty and most especially his desire to inspire others to serve, are powerfully evident in his famous poem. His dedication to his brothers-in-arms, his regiment (the Royal Regiment of Canadian Artillery) and his "beloved guns" (which represented that regiment for him) are likewise well-known. Indeed, many are familiar with the story of his resentment at being pulled from the front to serve in the medical corps. He disapprovingly declared, "All the goddam doctors in the world will not win this bloody war: what we need is more and more fighting men."

As a fellow officer of the Royal Regiment of Canadian Artillery, I understand the lure of *Ubique* and *Quo fas et gloria ducunt*, the mottoes of the regiment: "Everywhere" and "Whither Right and Glory Lead." Before Canada even existed (in fact, more than a hundred years before Confederation), the first company of the Artillery was formed here, and since that time its gunners have served at home and abroad in national emergencies, world wars and peacekeeping missions.

A few years ago, the senior officers of the Artillery gathered to discuss a plan to preserve our memorabilia and our history. As the longest-serving regiment, we had many important artifacts scattered across the country, from Victoria's coastal gun batteries to Halifax's Citadel, and an important history to tell. We wanted to launch a fundraising campaign to bring what we could together into one place, our home station, in Shilo, Manitoba.

At that meeting, I was called upon to articulate the need for this campaign to my fellow senior gunners. Off the top of my head, I began to speak about what the Artillery meant to me. I am no poet like Lieutenant-Colonel McCrae, but in that moment the words came to me with surprising ease, because I was speaking from my true, inner self. Being a soldier is not a profession for me, it is my life's meaning. It is me. Since the day I was born, to a Dutch war bride and a Canadian staff sergeant, through my childhood, playing with toy soldiers and growing up in military quarters and veterans' housing, through cadets, the reserves and military college, the army has seeped into my skin, colouring my soul khaki.

I began *Shake Hands with the Devil*, which is an account of my time in Rwanda, with, "My first love has always been the army. It has been my mistress, my muse and my family." While this may have startled civilian readers, as it likely did my wife and children, it is true, and I have no qualms admitting it. I am a living entity of the army, and I suspect many other soldiers feel the same.

In this spirit, speaking to my fellow officers that day, I recalled times in the midst of the Rwanda genocide when we were under imminent threat: my headquarters were under bombardment; we were expecting the extremists to come at any moment for the

Tutsis under our protection; there were no reinforcements, little ammunition—only a few rounds per soldier—and there were calls across the airwaves to "kill Dallaire" on sight.

As a soldier, in those moments of extremity, when the next bullet will likely be yours, you wonder what compels you to continue. I have puzzled over what forced me forward through the chaos and madness of the genocide. A sense of duty? My family, my flag, my brothers-at-arms? All of these were powerful motivations, rooted deeply in me, but were they the answer?

Duty was second nature, not a driving force; our training takes us beyond duty to a place where doing what we must do becomes instinctive. We live the unlimited-liability clause of our commitment to serve. My family was military born and bred; they knew the consequences of my serving in a war zone. My devotion to my country and my fellow soldiers was not what kept me from withdrawing when all seemed lost (even when I was ordered to do so), because my mission in Rwanda was not to defend my own but to protect the thousands of innocent strangers who were being so ruthlessly slaughtered.

No, what compelled me in Rwanda in those moments of dire danger was the thought of the corps, the fact that I was standing on the shoulders of those who had gone before me: the regiment, its spirit and what it had inculcated in me as an individual, its history and reputation. It was the secure place I held within my regimental family that compelled me to do my part in its honourable history. I would not break faith.

I had never articulated this before, and as I stood before my fellow gunner officers and the full weight of what I had experienced came crashing down on me, I had tears in my eyes. It was the first time over the many years since the genocide that I had acknowledged this most intimate link with the world outside of

The burden of command: King George V (left) at a makeshift Canadian cemetery, Vimy Ridge, July 1917.

that civil war zone. Although I knew the cavalry was not coming over the hill, I realized I did not stand alone. The generations who had faced adversity in combat were by my side, extending a steadying hand, reinforcing my will to fight.

McCrae is part of that family, that history, that regiment.

WHILE I RESPOND to "In Flanders Fields" most strongly as a gunner, I feel it most intimately as a field commander. Since frontline soldiers make the ultimate sacrifice in war, there has been very little written, in poetry or prose, of the "burden of command." And rightly so.

But for me, the veiled brutality of "In Flanders Fields"—the stark evidence that blood is shed and people die in war—also underlines the particular impact of war on those who command troops, who give the orders that put them in harm's way. It reveals the anguish commanders experience when they send soldiers to what may be their deaths.

As a commander, you strive to make your fighting unit as effective as possible; you nurture it through training, equipment and logistics. You carefully build cohesion, morale and group awareness, helping it to forge a superbly effective machine mandated to use disciplined force. You monitor and influence everything—from how your soldiers dress to their personal lives—so they may concentrate entirely on the mission. You protect them, engage them, work to improve their overall quality of life. You are building a unit that will fight to defeat the enemy and will pay the cost in human life once the unit is engaged. You articulate the mission, and you must sustain the effort to achieve it. And yet the construct of the army dictates that the person who shapes and builds the unit is also the one who will give the orders that may damage or destroy it.

A commander must suppress the pain of human loss and try to mitigate the destructive impact of battle on the unit. It is one thing to win your first engagement, but it's another to sustain the fight with the same spirit the unit had when it was whole. Once a unit has taken casualties, each soldier is psychologically affected. We use the terms "bloodied" or "battle-hardened" for soldiers and veterans who have, like McCrae, been forced to face this brutal reality. McCrae succeeded in articulating the price for the person who sent them into battle as much as for the frontline soldiers.

Since I came back from Rwanda, I have observed Remembrance Day not at the cenotaph but in private. To me, the day doesn't arouse remembrance but reality; it triggers the reliving of events just as fresh in my mind as the day they occurred. The price of having ordered men to their deaths, and of continuing to live with the fact that they are not alive today because of a decision I took, is a pain that never disappears, a wound that never heals. It is the price of command.

I don't talk about that much. No commander does.

EVERY YEAR, AT CANADIAN SCHOOLS, students prepare for November 11—the first, sometimes the only, exposure to the reality of fighting a war that many of them will ever have. They cut poppies out of construction paper, they recite or sing McCrae's century-old words, they try to stand silent for two interminable minutes.

But this act of commemoration reaches far deeper when Mom or Dad is in uniform or is a veteran, particularly if that parent is injured. When soldiers are deployed today, their families live the mission with them; between modern technologies and the news media, relatives are *au courant* within moments of events on battlefields halfway across the globe. When those family members read McCrae's poem, it is as real to them as it is to their loved ones overseas, for they are living the experience of having someone they love in harm's way.

Even harder for them is the fact that the whole country is *not* at war. Only those who are serving are. Civilians can easily forget that the Canadian Armed Forces have been in almost every war zone for the past twenty-five years, taking casualties, being shot at, shooting back. While Canada was at peace, the members of its armed forces were engaged on fields of battle far from home.

There is a powerful isolation in that fact for the children of serving men and women. "In Flanders Fields" can help relieve that isolation and bring its young readers into a community and a continuum of bravery and commitment. Such is the power of great poetry to mobilize emotion, empathy and courage.

BUT THE MOST PROFOUND impact of John McCrae's poem is that it can give us something around which we may unite. "In Flanders Fields" not only evokes emotion, it inspires collective resolve. We must each find our own meaning in it, our own place in its family of readers.

This poem is as pertinent now as it was at the height of the Great War. Unfortunately, there is enough evil in the world, and we are taking enough casualties, that McCrae's words still resonate deeply. Despite our peace, there are few who are entirely untouched by war. For those who are too young the poem may not bring to mind the blood-red flowers of France, or the green jungles of Rwanda, but its message of innocence lost may summon the clear blue sky over New York City on the September day that war came home.

The resolve that "In Flanders Fields" invokes is meant for all of us. Today's unfamiliar conflicts affect us all—though less overtly than did the First World War—even those of us who are not called. And for those of us who are, "In Flanders Fields" remains a rallying cry: "To you from failing hands we throw the torch." There is no question that McCrae is still calling us to duty.

It is up to us Canadians, and not just to our military men and women, to take up McCrae's torch. Not only to fight against sworn enemies but to protect innocents—even when no self-interest guides us.

Perhaps that torch is less metaphorical than it seems at first. Perhaps the torch we are passed can be more about spreading the light than taking up arms. Perhaps we are ready to use our hard-won wisdom and new technologies to resolve frictions and prevent conflicts from reaching catastrophic levels.

I believe if John McCrae were alive today, a hundred years after writing his extraordinary poem, he would engage with the same courage, commitment and self-sacrifice in the complex and ambiguous theatres of operations we now face around the globe. And he would find powerful language to inspire our commitment to the prevention of conflict by reminding us of fields now soaked in the blood of innocents.

Front cover of a memorial booklet (date unknown), *In Flanders Fields* by Lt. Col. John McCrae, M.D. and *America's Answer* by R.W. Lillard, *1914-1918*. McCrae's poem inspired others to write about the war, including Lillard's *America's Answer* and Moina Michael's *We Shall Keep the Faith*.

K. Colquhoun

TIM COOK
FORGED IN FIRE

John McCrae has been defined by his most famous poem, but this soldier, educator, doctor and poet was far more complex, and far more interesting, than this single work. Handsome, intelligent and passionate, he made friends easily, inspired those who met him and was a success in almost everything he did. He was described by one admirer, a doctor who served in the war with him, as a "rare humanist." His was a life defined by duty and hard work; he was a healer and a warrior. The Great War of 1914 to 1918, with its trauma and strain, both elevated John McCrae into a figure of world-wide renown and cut his life's work short.

CONSIDERING HIS FAMILY HISTORY, it's not surprising that John McCrae felt a deep connection to the military. A descendant of the Scottish clan known as the "Wild McCraes," his father, David, was four years old when his family emigrated to Canada in 1849. The Scottish Presbyterians sought prosperity through perseverance and work, and soon the McCrae family was in the lumber business, later running a successful woollen mill in Guelph, Ontario. After he graduated from the Ontario Veterinary College, David took over the business, but his first love was the military. He had been a member of the 47th Foot from the age of twenty, and the militia offered him an opportunity to combine patriotism and duty while chumming around

In 1894, McCrae graduated from the University of Toronto with a bachelor's degree in arts and languages. His professors suggested he pursue medicine.

with other like-minded young men and the elite who served as the regiment's officers. After qualifying to drill a company of infantry, David was one of the founders of Guelph's first militia artillery units and later commanded the 1st Brigade of Field Artillery.

John was born on November 30, 1872, in Guelph. In the family's stone cottage on Water Street, by the Speed River, John, his older brother, Thomas, and younger sister, Geills, grew up listening to their father's military stories, especially his role in repelling the American-Irish Fenian invasion of 1866. This personal history was infused with tales of how the British Empire was won through military might and, as many believed at the time, by extending a civilizing mission to those people under the protection of the Union Jack.

It was a natural step for John to join the Guelph Highland Cadet Corps at age fourteen in 1887. Through service in the military, even as a young man, he believed he could carry out his duty to Empire, Canada and community. His mother, Janet Simpson Eckford, was a voracious reader who ensured that studies came before drill. John—known as Jack to his friends and family—did both well. The handsome young man was a first-class student, with a stunning memory for poignant sayings and poetic stanzas. He was also an enthusiast for drill and bayonet practice, and when he was fifteen he won the gold medal for best-drilled cadet in Ontario.

Gifted in mind and agile in body, John was already close to six feet tall when at sixteen he became the first Guelph student to win a scholarship to enter the University of Toronto. He started university in 1888, where he studied the arts and languages, including Greek, Latin, French and German. The young scholar excelled at everything, but he was directed by his professors to specialize in medicine. It was not all books and studying—John also sang in the glee club, meeting the world with an infectious smile, crooked teeth and a ruddy complexion. The group performed throughout the campus and occasionally at the Toronto Lunatic Asylum, where, John wrote, "the audience was not disposed to be particularly critical." He enjoyed sports, but serious asthma held him back from playing too vigorously, and this condition plagued him to the point where he had to take a year off from his studies. While John was well-liked by his classmates, his Scottish Presbyterian upbringing made him frugal. His dowdy wardrobe was almost always out of fashion.

John remained deeply committed to the militia. In 1896, two years after graduating with his BA and halfway through a medical degree, he was commissioned as a lieutenant in No. 2 Battery of the 1st Brigade, Field Artillery, in Guelph. In 1898, he graduated with an honours degree in medicine from the University of Toronto, along with a gold medal for academic achievement as the top student. He soon set off for Baltimore, Maryland, to study with the world famous Canadian doctor William Osler. At Johns Hopkins Hospital, Osler taught his students to engage in the new medical revolution sweeping across the world in the late nineteenth century, which the doctor had a hand in codifying in his landmark text *The Principles and Practice of Medicine* (1892). The importance of antisepsis, higher quality X-rays, anaesthesia for longer surgeries and incorporating the enormous advances in anatomical knowledge and pathological treatment were all hallmarks of this medical age.

Having studied with the leading medical educator in the English-speaking world, John was granted a fellowship in pathology at McGill University in 1899. Confident in himself and his medical skills, he set off for a new phase of his life in Montreal, at the time Canada's largest and most glamorous city.

HALFWAY AROUND THE WORLD, in October 1899, the British Empire went to war against two small Boer republics in South Africa. There had been a long-simmering conflict between British imperialists in South Africa and the ultra-conservative Boers, but tension had grown in recent years over control of gold fields and enfranchisement for British citizens. This was the age when the British Empire covered one-fourth of the world, and Queen Victoria's sixty years of rule had been celebrated in the Diamond Jubilee of 1897. It was "The White Man's Burden," as Rudyard Kipling put it, to bring the supposedly civilizing rule of British law, rule and customs to every part of the British Empire. Few expected the world's greatest power to have trouble pacifying the republics. But no one told that to the tough Boer farmers.

After having carved out a homeland within southern Africa, the Boers had fought for their survival. And they were ready for battle. The Boer soldiers—divided into commando units that often rode scraggly ponies to navigate the harsh veld—inflicted several humiliating defeats on the British Army in seven days in December 1899 known as Black Week. Before this, however, London had sent out a call to its dominions to contribute fighting forces to the war effort, which was portrayed as a war of civilization and freedom rather than the imperial land grab that it was.

Dr. John McCrae, a healer, ached for war. He was desperate to enlist, even though he had recently taken up his fellowship at McGill. His family's history, his decade of service in the militia and a firm belief in the righteousness of Empire compelled him to put down scalpel and pick up the rifle. Yet he was not part of

McCrae in uniform, 1893.

the initial thousand soldiers of the Royal Canadian Regiment, 2nd Battalion, raised after October 13, 1899, when Prime Minister Sir Wilfrid Laurier's government allowed a battalion of volunteers to go overseas.

The almost twenty-seven-year-old John immediately regretted not enlisting. "I shall not pray for peace in our time," he wrote eagerly to his mother. "One campaign may cure me, but nothing else will, unless it should be old age. I regret bitterly that I did not enlist with the first, for I doubt if ever another chance will offer like it. This is not said in ignorance of what the hardships would be."

When the Laurier government announced a second contingent on December 21, John took temporary leave from his fellowship and enlisted as a lieutenant in the Royal Canadian Artillery, D Battery. There were 174 men and six guns. Lieutenant John McCrae was one of the three lieutenants in the battery, each of whom commanded two guns and a few dozen men. Much of the unit was recruited from McCrae's hometown of Guelph, where he returned to much fanfare. He and his fellow gunners were soon seen off by thousands of cheering and flag-waving Guelphites.

The second contingent of Canadians, consisting of mounted infantry and artillery, arrived in South Africa a few days before the Royal Canadian Regiment was engaged in the Battle of Paardeberg. That ten-day battle, starting on February 18, 1900, forced a Boer army to surrender, and the Canadians, who played a crucial part in the fighting, were celebrated throughout the Empire. Prime Minister Laurier, who had initially been reluctant to send an official Canadian contingent for fear of alienating Quebec, stood proudly in the House of Commons and proclaimed that a "new power had arisen in the West."

This was heady stuff for John and his men to follow. They found little glory on the empty veld, which John described as "God-forsaken." With the Boers wary of another major battle and instead conducting a guerilla campaign of hit and run, the British, Canadian and other forces from the Empire spent much of their time trying to corner the enemy. It was as much a war of the march as it was a war of the gun. On March 22, 1900, for instance, John noted in a letter that his gunners, who manned two 12-pounder artillery pieces and were attached to a mounted infantry unit, had trekked fifty-four miles in thirty-seven hours. The rocky scrubland was scalded by sun and blown with sandstorms. By day, the men sweated; by night, they froze. Swarms of flies harassed. Disease—especially typhoid fever—claimed thousands of British soldiers, far more than Boer bullets or shells. Water was always in short supply, and soldiers often survived by slurping from dirty shallow pools. "It is surprising how I can go without water," wrote John to his loved ones at home on April 10 after one ten-hour ride. "It is after nightfall that the thirst really seems to attack one and actually gnaws."

The rebel-hunting campaigns resulted in disease-plagued excursions from camps and bases. The Boers usually refused to face the Canadians except in the occasional ambush. More often, the soldiers of the Queen, trudging for kilometres across the veld, were forced to shoot their own emaciated horses that had been ridden into the ground. Only a few times during his year of service did Lieutenant John McCrae and D Battery find themselves in stand-up battles. On July 21, at De Wagendrift, a Boer force surprised a British train encamped, and McCrae's gunners were able to drive the Boers back with shellfire from about four thousand metres away. One of the Canadian lieutenants reported that the British regiments caught in the Boer shelling yelled in encouragement, "Give it to 'em, Canydians!" Another artillery duel in early September, at Lydenburg, lasted several hours. John was later to write, "The shrapnel burst all around us. I picked up a no. of falling pieces within a few feet of us. It was a trying afternoon . . . and we stood around & wondered if we would be hit." The British and Canadian gunners eventually got the upper hand and the Boers retreated. Except for a handful of short battles, John faced death most starkly when he crossed a river and his horse slipped, pinning him under the water. He came close to drowning before being pulled out from under the beast.

In the unforgiving campaign, morale sagged badly among the Canadian gunners, and especially in D Battery, where 80 per cent of the time was spent in garrison duty, guarding rail lines. It was a battle against boredom. John and his fellow officer Edward W.B. Morrison, an Ottawa journalist who would remain a lifelong friend, organized concerts, rifle shoots and sporting events to keep the rank and file occupied. His commanding officer described John as "an exceptionally clever officer and perfect gentleman." The ranks were just as effusive, with one of John's men writing that "the boys think he is alright. . . . The most popular officer of the lot." Good-tempered and always looking out for his men, John liked the rough gunners he commanded, almost all from the working class, although he noted with some surprise that "I always knew soldiers could swear, but you ought to hear these fellows." John won them over with a firm and fair hand and secretly took pleasure in keeping track of their salty sayings in a small notebook.

John was not disillusioned by the war, as some soldiers were, but neither did he glamourize it. He saw many deaths, especially from disease. In fact, when visiting a military hospital at De Aar, he was horrified by the terrible conditions in which the British soldiers suffered. "For absolute neglect and rotten administration, it is a model. I am ashamed of some members of my profession. Every day 15 to 30 Tommies die from fever or dysentery." John had been disgusted by the medical officers there, and he felt there was a "big breach" between them and the fighting men. He did not desire to be a hapless doctor in the military system. Despite the harsh nature of this mean little war, John wrote home that he "was getting used to soldiering and felt that he was born to do it."

JOHN RETURNED TO GUELPH and then Montreal as a hero in early 1901 and took up his fellowship. Of the 7,300 or so Canadians who served in the South African War, 89 were killed in action and 135 succumbed to disease before the Boers surrendered in 1902. Despite these losses, and the many thousands more to other soldiers and civilians, John believed the war had been worthwhile and wrote shortly after returning to Montreal that the Canadian sacrifice was evidence of a "voice of a new colony" that had been "won by blood." Nonetheless, he resigned his commission in 1904, his life increasingly busy with new medical postings and responsibilities. He had got that war out of his system, and now he was going to turn his sights to saving lives.

John was soon a successful pathologist in Montreal. He had his own private practice, and he accepted posts at the Royal Victoria Hospital and the Alexandra Hospital. Doctors commanded respect in society, but they did not make enormous salaries, and John lived on the top floor of a house owned by a friend and fellow doctor, Edward Archibald. He was known for treating the poor of Montreal and waiving his fees. His passion

McCrae (far right) with patients and student doctors at the
Alexandra Hospital, Montreal, 1910.

was in unlocking the mysteries of the body, and he continued to study pathogens, lung diseases and scarlet fever. Many of his patients were young children who succumbed to Montreal's dirty water and slum living. At the turn of the century, about one-fifth of all Montreal babies died before their first year. One of John's academic papers was entitled "An Analysis of Two Hundred Autopsies upon Infants."

Like all doctors, John necessarily hardened himself to loss and death. But he was never callous. He retained his easy ways, and this made him both a good companion to other physicians and an ideal instructor. He was also gentle with patients, having been trained to listen to their complaints in the hope of determining clues to their disease or ailment. In 1909, he began lecturing at McGill. The university's school of medicine was recognized as one of the finest in North America, and by all accounts John was an excellent professor. He taught bacteriology and pathology (the study of the body and organs to determine disease), and he was a specialist in infectious diseases like diphtheria and scarlet fever. Few students missed his lectures and autopsies, and he in turn took time from his busy schedule to inquire about their lives. One of the younger doctors who watched him instruct at the hospital and in the university, Oskar Klotz, admired John's knowledge and manner: "John McCrae was a born teacher. . . . The students loved him for the interest he always displayed in their difficulties and because he showed the human side of medicine."

When not teaching or treating the sick, John took up the pen. He had always dabbled in writing and poetry, having published stories with the University of Toronto student paper, the *Varsity*, and placing several poems in the Toronto *Globe*, *Canadian Magazine* and *Massey's Magazine* throughout the 1890s.

John was often drawn to dark topics. "The Song of the Derelict" (1898), which captured the power of the sea as witnessed on a doomed ship, contained the line "no pilot but Death at the rudderless wheel," while other poems, such as "Slumber Songs" (1897), were of fated romance and lovers divided by death.

In spite of his exceedingly busy schedule, John was a fixture in Montreal's writing scene. For his accomplished poetry, he was invited to join the Pen and Pencil Club. It was a select group of artists and writers—including Maurice Cullen, Robert Harris, William Van Horne, Stephen Leacock and Andrew Macphail—who met biweekly to read from their latest works or show their art. Macphail wrote impishly of the club, "It contained no member who should not be in it; and no one was left out who should be in. The number was about a dozen. . . . The place was a home for the spirit wearied by the week's work." John was a lifelong drawer, and he filled many sketchbooks, but his strength was in writing. He continued to publish poems during this period, trying out versions at the club and then usually finding a home for them in the influential *University Magazine*, a national journal of culture and opinion edited by his friend Macphail.

While many commented on John's good humour and mirthful approach to life, he had a darker side. He knew grief and death and had witnessed the loss of youth through war and disease. Many of his poems were themed around the search for peace and rest in the afterlife. "The Unconquered Dead," published in *University Magazine* in December 1905, is revealing of this dark strain.

". . . defeated, with great loss."

Not we the conquered! Not to us the blame
Of them that flee, of them that basely yield;
Nor ours the shout of victory, the fame
Of them that vanquish in a stricken field.

That day of battle in the dusty heat
We lay and heard the bullets swish and sing
Like scythes amid the over-ripened wheat,
And we the harvest of their garnering.

Some yielded. No, not we! Not we, we swear
By these our wounds; this trench upon the hill
Where all the shell-strewn earth is seamed and bare,
Was ours to keep; and lo! we have it still.

We might have yielded, even we, but death
Came for our helper; like a sudden flood
The crashing darkness fell; our painful breath
We drew with gasps amid the choking blood.

The roar fell faint and farther off and soon
Sank to a foolish humming in our ears,
Like crickets in the long, hot afternoon
Among the wheatfields of the olden years.

Before our eyes a boundless wall of red
Shot through by sudden streaks of jagged pain!
Then a slow-gathering darkness overhead
And rest came on us like a quiet rain.

Not we the conquered! Not to us the shame,
Who hold our earthen ramparts, nor shall cease
To hold them ever; victors we, who came
In that fierce moment to our honoured peace.

The dead are central to this poem and many others that sprang from John's imagination. They are not gone and forgotten, and they have done their duty. "Not to us the shame," John wrote of the fallen, but he was less sure about the living.

While poetry won John recognition in literary circles, he was a doctor first. He published a number of lauded medical articles, forty-six in total, and passed the membership examination to gain a coveted place in the Royal College of Physicians in London, England. He also wrote two textbooks. The better known manual was co-authored with Professor John Adami, *A Text-Book of Pathology for Students of Medicine* (1912). It was far from poetry, but McCrae's contribution was enough for Adami—his mentor and one of the most respected pathologists in the country—to label him "the most talented physician of his generation." The praise was, perhaps, an exaggeration, but there was no denying his skill as a physician and educator, and six years after the textbook's publication, one doctor wrote that it was "easily one of the best and most widely known" texts on pathology.

John read widely and travelled extensively. He had an affinity for ships and naval history. An outdoorsman, he was invited in 1910 to join the governor general of Canada, Earl Grey, on a canoe trip from Lake Winnipeg to Hudson Bay. After eleven days on the water, the expedition went by steamer around Newfoundland,

McCrae in 1912. He had written poetry since his university days, and his poems often explored themes of death and the subsequent peace of the afterlife.

visited the Maritime provinces and then returned to Quebec. John entertained his companions throughout the voyage. After the successful trip, Earl Grey wrote to him, "It was a great pleasure to have you as one of my party." Attesting to John's bonhomie, the governor general quipped, "You were able to beat the record of the *Arabian Nights* for I believe the 3,000 miles of our travel were illuminated by as many of your stories."

Stories were important to John, and he was comfortable in a crowd and usually at the centre of attention. He could spin a tale about soldiering for a group of men and find something very different for women. He was well read, versed in the arts and a recognized poet; at the same time, he could talk sports, fishing and travel. The doctor's gregarious nature brought unending invitations, and he was a member of many social clubs, including the University Club and the Montreal Military Institute. He retained his strong spiritual values and was an avid churchgoer, singing heartily the hymns at St. Paul's Presbyterian Church on Sherbrooke Street.

As a doctor, veteran and bon vivant, the handsome John McCrae—six feet tall, clean-shaven, strong-chinned and with a full head of hair—was popular with women. Even as he aged, he had a youthful quality and was sometimes mistaken for a student on the university campus. One admirer observed that McCrae liked the enthusiasm, manner and fashion of students, "and their youth was imputed to him." He outgrew his own university affectation of dressing shabbily and was now a dapper man about town. More than a few sought him out as a husband, and he had relationships with a number of women. He was discreet. And he never married.

—

EUROPE SLITHERED TOWARDS WAR in late July 1914, with Austria and Serbia in conflict over the assassination of Archduke Ferdinand a month earlier. The potentially small Balkan war became a general European war—through complicated alliance systems, hyper-nationalism, territorial ambitions, past grievances and future fears—and then a world war. By early August, Germany and Austria-Hungary, the Central Powers, were pitted against the allied forces of Russia, France, Belgium, Britain and their colonies and dominions. Other nations would soon join the war: most notably the Ottoman Empire on the side of the Central Powers, and Italy and the United States on the side of the Allies.

Canada went to war on August 4, 1914. As a British dominion, Canada had no control over its foreign policy. But this was a voluntary war, and individual Canadians would decide if they wished to serve King and country.

Even though John McCrae was old for soldiering at forty-one and a respected doctor, he felt compelled to serve. In early August, while attending a medical conference in Britain, John cabled the Department of Militia and Defence to offer his services. He rationalized his thinking in a letter home about the "terrible state of affairs": "I am going because I think every bachelor, especially if he has experience of war, ought to go." Perhaps most poignantly, he finished, "I am really rather afraid, but more afraid to stay at home with my conscience."

With tens of thousands queuing up at the armouries across the country, John called in a few favours. He contacted his South African War comrade Edward Morrison. Editor-in-chief of the *Ottawa Citizen* from 1898 to 1913, Morrison had in 1913 joined the Permanent Force as director of artillery and now commanded the 1st Brigade, Canadian Field Artillery. Morrison would find a spot for his old friend.

When John enlisted on September 22, Morrison wanted to give him command of one of the three batteries of six 18-pounder artillery guns in his brigade, but the doctor's age and lack of recent military experience made this impossible. Nonetheless, Morrison ensured that John would go overseas as brigade surgeon at the rank of major, and also as the second-in-command of the brigade. It was quite unorthodox, and it attests both to John's stature and the patronage-driven state of affairs in the newly formed Canadian Expeditionary Force (CEF). John took his command as brigade surgeon but refused to wear the Red Cross armband that identified him as a non-combatant. He also wore his revolver and sword. In his mind, he was a soldier first.

The First Contingent of the CEF went overseas in October 1914, more than 30,000 strong. They would be followed by close to another 600,000 citizen-soldiers who enlisted in the coming years or, after the Military Service Act was passed in late 1917, were forced by conscription into uniform. The First Contingent, from which the Canadian Division was formed, spent four months training on Salisbury Plain, until February 1915. Here, the soldiers learned rifle shooting and trench building, and marching in the mud. It rained 89 of 123 days, but morale remained high. Medical officers like John watched for outbreaks of disease that might decimate the Canadian troops, who were living under canvas in atrocious conditions for much of the time. Efficient medical services kept losses to a minimum.

John kept up his easy relationship with the rank and file in the 1st Artillery Brigade, which was largely drawn from Ottawa, Belleville, Gananoque and Kingston. One gunner, C.L.C. Allinson, recounted how two of the rougher men in the brigade, experienced drivers who worked in lumber camps, had gone on leave with all their money. Their drunken exploits had got them thrown in jail, and they were brought back to the camp to receive further punishment. Under guard, the two drivers were going to miss the turkey Christmas dinner. McCrae had his medical corporal send over to the prisoners two small bottles containing a dark-brown liquid. The bottles were labelled To Be Taken Before Meals. It was army rum. One can imagine the smile on the prisoners' faces when they uncorked their medicine. The story made the rounds and only added to John's already sterling reputation among the men.

THE CANADIAN DIVISION, some eighteen thousand strong, went to France in February 1915. The opening phase of the war in the west had seen Germany invade Belgium, with its armies sweeping southward into France. Belgian, French and British troops were pushed back on the Western Front, but both sides had fought ferociously, and hundreds of thousands of dead soldiers were left rotting in the open fields. Soldiers dug into the ground to escape the murderous firepower of machine guns and artillery, and the ditches were soon deepened to trenches. By the end of 1914, the trenches ran from Switzerland to the North Sea, some seven hundred kilometres, with the German army occupying most of Belgium and the northeast of France. These underground cities were crude, muddy and filthy, but the soldiers would call them home for much of the next four years.

"Most of the trench injuries are of the head, and therefore there is a high proportion . . . killed in the daily warfare as opposed to an attack," John wrote to his mother. "Our Canadian plots fill up rapidly." The daily shelling of the trenches, and the enemy's snipers who waited for careless men to show their heads above the sandbags, led to mass death. As the Canadians were cycled into the trenches on four- to six-day tours, starting in late February, they steadily lost soldiers. Within six weeks, 278 men were killed and wounded.

The guns of the 1st Brigade were situated a few thousand metres to the rear of the front lines, and there were few gunners lost at this stage in the war. Instead, the guns on both sides targeted the enemy's trenches. The hurricane bombardments of tens of thousands of shells that were common after 1916 were also absent due to shell shortages. The 1st Brigade's guns fired only about a dozen shells a day in early 1915, but there was much activity in support of the British offensive at Neuve Chapelle, in the Artois region of France, on March 10. With increased shell stockpiles for the battle, the unit's war diary reported, "Brigade salvos fired at 5 minute intervals followed by battery salvos in echelon. Infantry officers in trenches reported fire very effective. In no case did our shell[s] endanger our trenches although 80 yards apart in some paces. German battery 800 yards S.E. from our line was shelled by our batteries. Enemy's battery ceased fire." The British made little progress in driving the Germans back and suffered about 11,600 British and Indian casualties.

IN EARLY APRIL, the Canadians moved to the Ypres front in Belgium. It was here, in the fields of Flanders, where the Canadians would fight in their first major battle of the war. The ground to the east of Ypres, the last major Belgian town retained by the Allies, had been the scene of brutal fighting in October and November 1914. The First Battle of Ypres saw the French, British and Belgians attempt to block the German thrust through the town of Ypres and then on to the Channel ports on the coast. The casualties reached staggering heights: about 50,000 French, 21,500 Belgians and 55,000 British were killed or wounded. In turn, the Allies inflicted about 135,000 casualties on the German forces. Thousands of maggot-ridden bodies lay where they fell, slowly consumed by the earth or mulched by indiscriminate shellfire. The sickly sweet stench from the decomposing dead hung in the air for several kilometres.

The Allies held a salient that extended five miles west from the Yser Canal in a deep curve into the German lines. Behind the canal, in Allied territory, was the moated town of Ypres, with its majestic Cloth Hall. Six Allied divisions were in the front lines of the salient, which ran some seventeen miles from end to end. But because the front jutted into the enemy lines, it was surrounded on three sides by the Germans. With such a position, the enemy guns could fire freely into the rear areas. No one was safe. There had been talk of pulling back to the Yser Canal, but Allied high command refused to give up more ground to the Germans. The Canadians had been ordered "to hold the front trenches at all costs, and, in the event of any trench being lost, to counter-attack at once."

While the Germans were outnumbered on the Western Front, they planned a sharp attack at Ypres to throw back the Allies and to cover the movement eastward of a number of divisions to shore up the Eastern Front war against the Russians. Throughout the winter, they had marched reserves to the Ypres Salient to amass overwhelming firepower and troops in time for a spring offensive. The Second Battle of Ypres began on April 22 when the Germans unleashed a heavy bombardment against the Allied lines, held by French colonial, British and Canadian troops. Belgian civilians in the town of Ypres were targeted as high-calibre shells rained down, shattering stone and ending lives. Ypres burned, and the gothic Cloth Hall was steadily reduced by shellfire and flames. In the late afternoon of that sunny, warm day, the Germans released 160 tons of lung-searing chlorine gas from 5,730 large metal cylinders. It was the first large-scale release of lethal gas in the history of warfare.

In the face of the deadly greenish-yellow cloud, which extended some six kilometres across, two French colonial divisions—45th Algerian and 87th French Territorial—suffocated or fled. The Canadian units in the front lines to the right of them hacked through some of the lethal vapour but did not encounter the densest part of the cloud. The Canadians shifted over to cover the gap in the left flank of Allied lines and, knowing the situation was desperate, counterattacked. An aggressive Canadian bayonet charge against Germans in Kitcheners Wood and later against Mauser Ridge slowed the enemy advance. By the second day of battle, most of the Canadian division had been rushed forward into combat. The next four days would be among the most costly of the war for the Canadians.

Major John McCrae watched the disaster unfold from behind the front lines. John's artillery brigade was situated on the west bank of the Yser Canal, with the other two brigades of the Canadians' guns to the east of the canal, closer to the front lines. He witnessed the retreating French soldiers who had been gassed, and he agonized over the thousands of Belgian civilians streaming from the burning town of Ypres. John wrote in his diary, in the form of a letter to his mother, "Of one's feelings all this night—of the asphyxiated French soldiers—of the women and children—of the cheery steady British reinforcements that moved up quickly past us, going up, not back—I could write, but you can imagine."

With the frontline infantry outnumbered and shelled relentlessly, the Canadian gunners played a crucial role in holding off the German troops. The 18-pounder artillery piece fired a shell of that weight containing high explosives and shrapnel. At this stage in the war, however, high-explosive shells were few, and the Canadian gunners relied on shrapnel. The shell—about as long as a man's forearm—could be fired around six thousand metres and was timed with a fuse to explode above the enemy position, showering it with hundreds of metal ball bearings and fragments from the exploding steel casing. Flesh was shredded under this shotgun-like blast. Troops in trenches were generally safe, as the shells had to explode at a perfect spot to hail down on the underground positions, but soldiers advancing in the open suffered heavily.

It was the Canadians who were outgunned during the battle. The Germans had grouped a heavy concentration of artillery pieces, including 147 siege guns that delivered devastating bombardments. The air was heavy with metal. McCrae was to write, "Gunfire and rifle fire never ceased 60 seconds—and behind it all was the constant sights of the dead and wounded, the maimed and the terrible anxiety lest the line should give way."

For most of the battle, John operated on wounded men who passed through his rough surgical room carved into the side of a hill. Essex Farm bunker was a muddy cave reinforced with wood and buttressed by a small sandbag wall to the rear to prevent back-blast of shrapnel from passing through the entrance into his operating room. A crude table was soon occupied by the bleeding and broken. Straw soaked up the blood. The steady thump of shellfire shook his dugout, and dust and debris filtered down on the doctor and his patients. John operated, tied off arteries, sewed up flesh. There were no blood transfusions at this point in the war, and most of his pain medication, primarily morphine, was rapidly used up. He saved dozens of soldiers' lives over the coming days, but he also agonized as men bled out and slipped into shock, or were carried in with mangled bodies too badly shattered to heal.

One of John's former students, and a pre-war colleague at the Royal Victoria, Francis Scrimger, was a fellow medical officer at the front. Bespectacled and slight, Scrimger did not look like a soldier, but, like John, he hurled himself into action, assisting the wounded in the 14th Battalion. Scrimger was closer to the front than John was, and he raced forward to care for those men who could not be carried to the rear. All through April 23, Scrimger dressed wounds, only taking a few minutes to jot notes in his diary about the sights that he and other medical doctors witnessed: "There were some bad wounds— legs and arms crushed and heads torn open—but very few of the abdomen and chest." Those men with wounds to the chest and abdomen were almost always doomed to a rapid death, and stretcher-bearers rarely carried them back over hundreds of metres of broken ground to be seen by doctors. Scrimger, on April 24, was aware that there were wounded men in the front lines, and he went forward to care for them. In one heroic action, his makeshift surgical area there was overrun by Germans, and he carried a burly soldier on his back out of danger. For his bravery throughout the battle and for that specific action, he was awarded the Empire's highest gallantry award, the Victoria Cross.

At the front or rear, the Canadians were shelled non-stop. Corpses piled up on the battlefield. Some were cleaved in two or missing limbs. Others were killed without visible wounds, usually from a high-explosive blast that destroyed internal organs. John spent much of his time caring for the wounded, but he needed occasional breaks, and he took them behind a small ridge about twenty feet high near the canal. It offered protection from the shells and a chance to reflect upon what he'd witnessed. "I saw one bicycle orderly: a shell exploded and he seemed to pedal on for eight or ten revolutions and then collapsed in a heap—dead." There was nothing John could do for him, and he remained unburied for some time.

Soon all the nearby farms and windmills were shelled. The burning structures added an apocalyptic glow to the battlefield. On April 24, the Germans unleashed a second gas attack against the Canadian lines. The cloud was smaller than the first but much more dense. The choking and hacking Canadians masked their faces with clothes doused with water and urine to cut some of the chlorine, but many succumbed. The Canadians were pushed back, but they did not break.

James Walker, of No. 2 Canadian Stationary Hospital, described the gassed Canadians who made their way back to his medical unit: "The deadly gas which had been pressed into use so effectively by the enemy had told the ghastly tale. Staggering, dumbfounded and stupefied they were brought in, after having been conveyed from the ambulance train. . . . The effect of these gas fumes which wrought such deadly havoc is a noticeable watery running of the eyes. Later the features become discoloured by a sort of green and yellowish hue. Many took the precautions to stuff handkerchiefs in their mouths. However, once too much gas has been inhaled its action has the same effect upon the lungs as a slow process of drowning." John, too, worked in the poisonous vapours, which did nothing good for his asthmatic lungs. "One's eyes smarted," he wrote, "and breathing was very laboured."

The Canadian infantry were finally relieved throughout April 25 and 26, after four days of battle in which more than six thousand men were killed, wounded or captured. The artillery and medical units were not so lucky. They continued to support the other Allied troops in the line. The war diary for the 1st Brigade noted that from its unit three men were killed and thirty wounded by April 27, with the numbers jumping to forty-six casualties on April 29. The next day, the gunners supported a French attack. One eyewitness wrote rather laconically, "A few German prisoners were taken but as a rule no quarter was given."

Amid this horror, John noted in his diary the oddness of the nearly continuous enemy bombardment—the tremors and clashes, along with the screams of the wounded—contrasting with how the "birds sing in the trees over our heads." Weary and worn, the surgeon struggled to keep his composure under the strain, and he wrote of his "mixture of anger and apprehension." After days of shelling and lack of sleep, John lost his appetite, but he forced himself to eat, aware that his body needed the sustenance. The death of so many friends, comrades and countrymen haunted him, and he wrote that "the general impression in my mind is of a nightmare."

ON MAY 2, after nearly ten continuous days of shell strafing, during which John wrote that "we really expected to die," the exhausted surgeon was informed that one of his friends in the brigade, twenty-two-year-old Lieutenant Alexis Helmer, a blue-eyed and fair-haired leader, had been killed around 8 a.m. A shell had dismembered his body to the point where the pieces were collected and buried in a few sandbags sewn together in an army blanket. A distraught John officiated at Helmer's hastily arranged funeral a few hours later. With all the chaplains busy burying other men, John gave the Church of England's "Order of Burial of the Dead" from memory and said goodbye. Along with the bags of bloody remains was a picture of Helmer's fiancée.

Sometime on May 2, after burying Helmer, John began composing his famous poem "In Flanders Fields." The story of the poem's origins is not entirely clear, and John did not care enough to record it for posterity. He appears to have written it on May 2 and 3 in a quiet spot near his dugout and within sight of a cemetery containing French and, more recently, Canadian dead, where there were rows upon rows of crosses and red poppies emerging from the soil. Having composed a version of the poem on the second, he played around with it in his head and experimented with the metre, and on the third the words rushed out of him in a cathartic release over twenty minutes.

It was done. Having written the sixteen-line poem on a piece of wrapping paper, John put it aside and got on with the battle. Later, on the encouragement of a few friends who read it over, he submitted it to the English magazine the *Spectator*. It was rejected. John seems to have continued tinkering with the poem and submitted again with the famous satirical magazine *Punch*. "In Flanders Fields" was published anonymously in those pages on December 8, 1915. It took some time for it to be revealed that it had come from John McCrae.

"HOW TIRED WE ARE! Weary in body and wearier in mind," John wrote in his diary in the aftermath of the Second Battle of Ypres, still wearing uniform and boots that were stained with the blood of others. The battle had etched itself deep into him. He was changed from the ordeal—he described it as "17 Days of Hades"—and when he and his fellow gunners were finally pulled

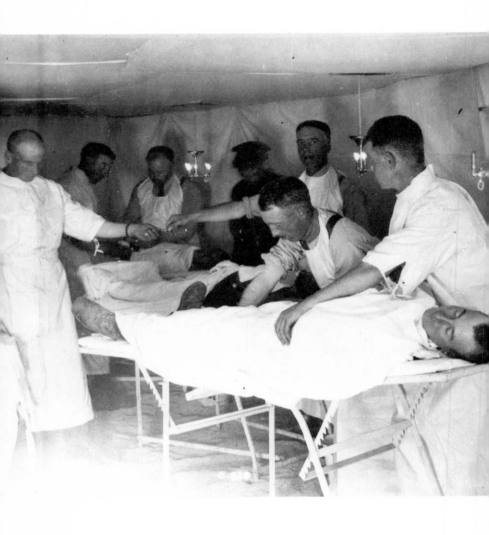

Operating tent of the 3rd Field Ambulance Dressing Station, Vlamertinghe, Belgium, August 1916. Note the absence of surgical masks or gloves.

from the line on May 9, he could scarcely believe he had survived. The 1st Artillery Brigade had suffered at least seven killed and sixty-one wounded, with five of the twelve guns destroyed.

In the aftermath of Ypres, John was ordered to leave the artillery and join the Canadian Army Medical Corps. Even worn out and in need of a rest, he was not happy with being struck off strength from the 1st Brigade. As he was saying goodbye to his comrades, he lamented to one of them, "All the goddam doctors in the world will not win this bloody war: what we need is more and more fighting men." That was indeed true, but someone would have to sustain and heal those men when they were injured. By war's end, half of all Canadian doctors served overseas, leaving a shortage in the Dominion and especially in rural areas.

On June 1, 1915, John McCrae—soon to be promoted to lieutenant-colonel—moved to the not-yet-formed No. 3 Canadian General Hospital (McGill), staffed largely by students, nurses and colleagues from his university. The hospital of 1,040 beds, which took its first patients in August, was located at Dannes-Camiers, on the north French coast. At the time, No. 3 Canadian Hospital consisted of fifty-five large marquees—coloured cotton tents decorated with elaborate Oriental designs and housing more than fifty beds each—that had been presented by the viceroy of India. There were close to two hundred other tents for all other aspects of the medical work, from surgical rooms to an X-ray centre, and also to house doctors, orderlies and nurses. John was the officer in charge of medicine, a senior medical and administrative position in which he commanded many of his old friends.

Within a month of opening on August 8, the hospital was admitting hundreds of patients daily. The doctors, surgeons and nurses on staff operated on and cared for the patients, but most of the wounded were sent on to Britain to clear space for the never-ending flow of soldiers from the trenches. One of the medical orderlies wrote in his diary during the Battle of Loos that autumn, "This week—the busiest since we opened—is a confusion to me of blood, gaping wounds, saline, and bichloride. Few particular events remain clearly in my mind."

Far from the battlefront, John agonized over the fact that he was safe from the danger. He was rarely seen to smile. One nurse who knew him in Montreal thought he had aged fifteen years, "his face lined and ashen grey in colour, his expression dull, his action slow and heavy." Another doctor, Harvey Cushing, from Harvard, wrote of John that "since those frightful days [of the Second Battle Ypres] he has never been his old gay and companionable self, but rather has sought solitude." John had left part of himself at Ypres.

As a senior medical administrator, he spent his time dealing with his medical staff and patients. "My duties are so multifarious that I find it hard to get them done." He pushed himself hard, monitoring thirty to forty patients a day in his rounds of the lung ward, where he cared for men with infections and pneumonia as well as wounds to the chest from shrapnel or poison gas. He also drove his doctors and nurses. He was a demanding disciplinarian, ensuring that minor rules and regulations were followed. Some of his pre-war friends were surprised and even a little hurt by John's insistence on military discipline, and his mentor and friend John Adami, who served overseas in a number of administrative roles during the war, recounted that "not all at first understood the change or could rise to his level of service." Yet this was one way to remain a soldier in the medical war, although he no doubt also remembered the terrible hospital system in South Africa, where through neglect and unprofessionalism patients died unnecessarily. Under John's watch, the same would not occur.

Despite his fame due to "In Flanders Fields," he frequently refused invitations to travel to London, where he would have been feted. He seemed to want to punish himself for not being at the front, within the sound of the guns, and perhaps for his own monumental success. He frequently isolated himself from his colleagues. Unlike before the war, he had difficulty enjoying idle conversation. Instead, he tended to his patients, read deeply and wrote to his family at home, including twice-weekly letters to his mother. His lifelong interest in animals allowed him to find solace in several pets. And during stressful periods at the hospital, he took to the French countryside with his dog, Bonneau, and his trusted horse, Bonfire.

In the harsh winter of 1915–1916, the hospital, having been twice ravaged by storms that blew down the tents, was finally moved to an abandoned Jesuit college northeast of Boulogne. It was operational again by February 1916, with an increased capacity of more than 1,500 beds. No. 3 Canadian Hospital almost immediately resumed taking in hundreds of patients daily. Many suffered from trench foot. Soldiers forced to stand in slushy water for hours on end in the trenches suffered frostbite and circulation problems. Serious cases saw feet swell, with gangrene setting in. Toes often had to be amputated by the time the patients were seen by doctors. John's hospital treated two hundred cases of trench foot in British soldiers in March 1916, and John made a study of them and possible forms of treatment, including wrapping affected feet in hot cloths and injecting them with a mild astringent.

Despite his important work, John remained uneasy at being away from the front lines and feared that he had dodged his duty as a soldier. Once, a patient called out to him, "Doctor," and he snapped back angrily, "Don't call me doctor. I'm as much a soldier as you are." Sir Andrew Macphail wrote of one conversation with his brooding friend during the terrible slaughter of the Battle of the Somme, from July to November 1916, which saw more than a million German, French, British and dominion troops killed and wounded. In a two-week period, No. 3 Canadian Hospital was inundated with 4,600 wounded soldiers, who were operated on and cared for before most of the cases were sent on to Britain for long-term recovery. As John saw the avalanche of wounded from the battle, he told Macphail that he felt like a deserter for not having left his body "upon the field along with friends of a lifetime."

Conflicted, tired and emotionally worn, John struggled with his temper, which he had rarely revealed before the war. In one unguarded letter, he wrote, "One feels a kind of blind anger which one cannot vent upon anyone." Another pre-war Montreal friend, now serving with No. 3 Canadian Hospital, Edward Archibald, observed that in the year since the Second Battle of Ypres, John had trouble concentrating and was often plagued by a lack of energy. With all the evidence of an internal struggle, it seems clear that McCrae was suffering from post-traumatic stress disorder, even though that term would not come into use for another sixty years. At the time, PTSD was known as shell shock. Soldiers suffering from unending strain broke down under the pressure. Men had trouble concentrating, lost their temper easily and developed physical tics and stutters. Nightmares hounded them. More serious cases, usually after a traumatic trigger event, such as seeing a friend killed or having a close call with death, resulted in a complete breakdown. Some men developed paralyzed limbs, others lost their minds. It was an ongoing challenge for the medical community to diagnose and treat the shell-shocked men, and methods of treatment ranged from Freudian discussions and rest to electroshock therapy and shaming. John pushed through the stress and strain, and after about a year Archibald observed that his nerves had calmed down and he was looking better.

John continued to find solace in his poetry. Before the war, the jovial doctor was drawn to dark poetry; after the Second Battle of Ypres, dark poetry poured forth from a dark man. While his poetry never defined him, he turned to it to make sense of his war experience. In June 1917, his second most famous poem, "The Anxious Dead," was published in the *Spectator*.

O guns, fall silent till the dead men hear
Above their heads the legions pressing on:
(These fought their fight in time of bitter fear,
And died not knowing how the day had gone.)

O flashing muzzles, pause, and let them see
The coming dawn that streaks the sky afar;
Then let your mighty chorus witness be
To them, and Caesar, that we still make war.

Tell them, O guns, that we have heard their call,
That we have sworn, and will not turn aside,
That we will onward till we win or fall,
That we will keep the faith for which they died.

Bid them be patient, and some day, anon,

They shall feel earth enwrapt in silence deep;

Shall greet, in wonderment, the quiet dawn,

And in content may turn them to their sleep.

As in "In Flanders Fields," the dead are the central actors; they have sacrificed all in battle and do not even know if their side has carried the day. The war has swept on, and now it is the survivors who must fight "onward till we win or fall." Again, it is the living who must keep faith with the fallen. Yet now John urges the dead to find solace in their "silence deep" in the "earth enwrapt." They have earned their rest. John, sadly, never felt he had earned the same relief.

THROUGHOUT 1917, the Allied armies in the east and west suffered catastrophic defeat or pyrrhic victories at the cost of hundreds of thousands of lives in recapturing a few more kilometres of chewed-up farmers' fields. The Arras and Passchendaele offensives by the British Expeditionary Force achieved few victories, while much of the French army was in mutiny after the ceaseless slaughter. In that same terrible year, the Russians withdrew from the war as civil war between Bolsheviks and anti-communists tore the country apart. There appeared to be no end in sight.

John cared for the thousands of bloodied and broken Canadians who passed through his hospital during the gutwrenching battles of Vimy, Hill 70 and Passchendaele. By the end of 1917, more than 30,000 Canadians had been killed and close to 100,000 wounded in body, mind and spirit. With the Belgian and French farmers' fields manured with human and animal waste for centuries, almost all of the soldiers' wounds were infected as bullets and shrapnel ripped through filthy clothing and carried dirt into flesh. With the wounded usually taking several days to reach the hospitals on the coast, some of the infections were beyond treating. One of the senior Canadian doctors testified, "I have seen cases in the Operating Room in which the tissue are so rotten with infection that portions of muscle tissue can be removed by the handful."

"Words fail me to describe how I hate Germany," wrote John. He had seen too much death. In early January 1918, one of his friends met him and was shocked by his physical and mental decline; he characterized him as "silent, asthmatic, moody." His audible wheeze had returned, and then on January 24 it deepened into a deep, rasping cough. John took to his bed. Despite close supervision and care, a fever came over him, and on January 28 the forty-five-year-old McCrae developed meningitis and slipped into a coma. The end came quickly, and he died in the early afternoon. It was five days after he had received the promotion to consulting physician for First British Army, the first Canadian to hold such a position.

His death was a shock to his friends, students and fellow healers on the Western Front and in Montreal and Guelph, as well as to millions in the English-speaking world. On January 29, John's funeral, along the coast at Wimereux, France, was attended by senior Canadian and British officers, including the Canadian Corps commander, Sir Arthur Currie; McGillites in uniform; and some 175 medical personnel. The hospital's nurses wore their long blue coats and white veils. His loyal horse, Bonfire, was attired in white ribbon, with John's boots placed traditionally reversed in the stirrups. Lieutenant-General Currie eulogized that John was "a soldier from top to toe: how he would have hated to die in bed." A wreath of hand-made poppies was placed on his coffin as it was lowered into the ground.

McCrae's funeral procession, Wimereaux, France, January 1918. A wreath of poppies decorates the coffin.

JOHN McCRAE'S POEM mattered far less to him than it did to others. He never lost his head over the fame. Duty was more important: to country, to comrades and to patients. Yet "In Flanders Fields" has lived on in memory and myth. The symbol of the passing torch resonated first in war and then in peace. A generation of grieving parents, grandparents and children, of weeping parishes and wasted communities, all sought meaning in the war that had so profoundly scarred the world. Was the Great War, with its nine million dead, a senseless slaughter? Many believed that. But not all, and perhaps not even the majority of Canadians. In the decade after the war's cessation on November 11, 1918, Canada's sacrifice of more than sixty thousand dead was remembered, reimagined and forged to mean something different across the Dominion. The survivors built several thousand memorials to the men who had marched away and never returned. Armistice Day—and, after 1931, Remembrance Day—was marked with two minutes of silence and red poppies. The dead were portrayed as having fallen during a just war for civilization. Their lives had not been lost in vain. And during that decade and those that followed, countless Canadians were joined by millions around the world who returned to John McCrae's words to soothe their scars and light the way forward.

A hundred years later, "In Flanders Fields" is still relevant. It is a cry from the heart that emerged during the wreckage of war. Yet its powerful words transcend the Great War; and John McCrae's rich life, as a man guided by scholarship, empire, war, art, education and medicine, also shines a light on what motivated the more than 620,000 Canadians who served and sacrificed, and those who continue to do so for the causes they believe in.

NOTE ON SOURCES

John McCrae's archival papers are held by the Guelph Museum and the Library and Archives of Canada in Ottawa (MG 30 D209). Excerpts from the letters written to his mother during the South African War were published in the *Evening Mercury* (Guelph, Ont.) between January and December 1900.

There are a number of histories documenting McCrae's life. The best is Diana Graves' *A Crown of Life: The World of John McCrae* (St. Catharines: Vanwell Pub., 1997). A little dated now, but still useful, is John Prescott's *In Flanders Fields: The Story of John McCrae* (Erin, 1985) and John M. Bassett's *John McCrae* (Markham: Fitzhenry & Whiteside, 1983). A. E. Byerly's *The McCraes of Guelph* (Elora, 1932) documents the McCrae family. A useful book for younger readers is Linda Granfield's *Remembering John McCrae: Soldier, Doctor, Poet* (Toronto: Scholastic Canada, 2009).

Tim Cook's *At the Sharp End: Canadians Fighting the Great War, 1914–1916* and *Shock Troops: Canadians Fighting the Great War, 1917–1918* provide an overview of the Canadian Corps in battle. R.C. Fetherstonhaugh's *No.3 Canadian General Hospital (McGill), 1914–1919*, (Montreal, 1928) situates McCrae and his medical work.

The most complete collection of McCrae's poetry was published *In Flanders Fields and Other Poems* (Toronto and New York, 1919). It also includes a long, personal and idiosyncratic article on McCrae by Sir Andrew Macphail entitled "An essay in character."

Overleaf: Mary Riter Hamilton, "The Sadness of the Somme," 1919. Hamilton spent three years touring the remains of Western Front battlefields, painting on everything from plywood to cardboard. She would eventually produce over 300 images and be awarded France's *Ordre des Palmes Académique* (Order of Public Instruction), the only Canadian war artist so honoured.

PATRICK LANE
THE WARS

I WAS EIGHT YEARS OLD in 1947 when my mother took off her poppy at the cenotaph on Remembrance Day and dropped it at her feet in the crushed snow. My memory of it is so clear. My father was marching away with the soldiers through the gates of the park, the bagpipes were howling, the snare drums rattling, and the people who had stood in the snow with heads bowed shuffled away, hunched in their coats on a cold November day. I was still standing at attention like my father told me to. I wanted to pick the poppy up, but I had to wait until the end. Then my mother pulled me away, her hand gripping the collar of my jacket.

Hours later, at twilight, I stood near the cenotaph at the edge of the beaten snow where the crowds had been, my eyes casting among the shadows, looking for what my mother had thrown away. I had no business being out in the cold with night coming on. I should have been home, the wood stove behind me throwing off heat, the kettle simmering, my mother making supper for us all.

It happened a long time ago.

IF I CLOSE MY EYES I can look back seventy years and see myself not at the cenotaph but in the warm kitchen in the house on Schubert Street when I was a boy in Vernon, in the Okanagan Valley. It is afternoon and I am kneeling on a wooden chair,

The cenotaph, City Hall, Toronto, November 1922.

59

leaning out over our rickety kitchen table, drawing on flattened sheets of brown grocer's paper. Under my hand a line of Sherman tanks advances across the brown paper field near a place my father called Nijmegen. I'd heard him speak of the battle only once, to Mr. Steinhoff, a man he had fought beside in the tank corps. They were standing in the back yard by the gate. I was in the woodshed, hidden by the door. My father never talked about the war to me or to my brothers, no matter our begging. I loved the sound of the word he spoke, Nijmegen, and tried to imagine what it had been like to be there.

The guns I draw shoot flares of red and yellow flame. I colour them with the stubs of crayon I take from a chipped Mason jar. Yellow and red, purple and blue, those are the colours of the guns when they fire, the arc of their flames the same as I'd seen in burning pits and bonfires, wood stoves and coal oil lamps. I draw my father standing in the turret of the lead tank, pointing across the river at the Germans. The enemy waits in staggered trenches on the other side of the bridge.

The tanks are ones I've seen in photographs in Liberty and Life. As I draw, I make the sounds of battle under my breath, the crash, smash, bang and roar of guns and armour, the groans and wails of dying men. I think I know what they sound like. I have learned to scream perfectly as I fall wounded and dying in the games of war I play with my brothers and friends in the hills above the town. It is what we always play, war.

My mother is behind me, bending over the pine boards my father nailed together as a counter for her by the galvanized tub we use as a sink. She scrapes carrots and peels potatoes, the rinds and skins scaling off in curls into a dented pail, where they will be saved and later boiled for soup. Nothing is wasted, nothing is thrown away. Not a curled slice of potato, parsnip, beet or carrot skin. Not a bit of gristle, not the skins of chickens or pigs, the neck, the liver, heart or kidneys of animals and birds, the fretted bones of a trout. There is not a shirt in the house where I live that cannot be mended, not a sock that can't be stretched over a darning egg. There's always a needle to nose its way among the thin threads of a worn heel, the weave of cotton or wool, to bind older threads together so that socks can be worn again and again until they are worn away entirely, each heel a spiderweb, a bit of gauze masquerading as a sock. Pants will be patched upon patches, collars and cuffs turned, elbows replaced, hems lifted to hide frays of cotton and wool, all repaired that is worn or torn. *Things need to be put back together*, is what my mother says. *We don't throw anything away around here.*

I am deep inside the war I am drawing. I don't hear my mother's paring knife or the snap and crackle of the wood burning in the stove. I don't notice my father being gone. He is at the Legion. A fire burns behind me. The brown paper rustles. My small hands draw the advancing tanks, the ones called Shermans, the ones my father drove in the war.

WHEN MY MOTHER WAS DYING in the hospital in Vancouver, I sat with her late into the night and we had long, disjointed exchanges that wandered back over the years. Her gesture toward conversation was a monologue, her mind going over the times of her century, the twentieth. She was not so much selfish as she was preoccupied with issues and ideas that had dominated her life. Her focus was sharp as ever, but she often went adrift, her reveries ranging across past slights and wounds, but triumphs too. There were her victories over the childhood abuse by her father; her struggles as a miner's wife in the Depression and as a soldier's wife living in poverty during the Second World

War; the early death of her eldest son, my brother, and the murder of her husband, my father, both of them gone in the troubled decade our family went through in the sixties. I listened to her as best I could, though at times I too drifted away, her monologues the modest ravings of the dying mother I loved. No matter the occasional excesses, the criticisms, the eighty-two-year-old woman on the bed was as feisty as ever, her eyes shining with the bright intensity the eyes of the dying often have. At times she seemed to smoulder inside, her memories dark flames no one—not even a god—could quite extinguish. It is as if the old know things we don't or can't imagine.

One night close to her passing she had been unusually quiet, the three other women in her room in extended care asleep in their beds. It was late and dark, with only an oblique shaft of light coming in from the hall. I listened to the sounds of the city in the distance, the last cars and trucks rumbling on Broadway, a taxi going up Cambie Street ferrying someone home to bed, and every once in a while the moan of a ship out in the harbour, one or more of the other ships answering it, a dense fog having rolled in from the Salish Sea. The ships' cries were unearthly and yet oddly reassuring, Leviathans singing ancient songs to each other in the mist. Earlier my mother and I had been speaking of the war, and the many anecdotes and stories had silenced us both. I remembered those times as mostly happy ones, but I was a child, and what does a child know of his parents' grief and desolation? In the theatre of my childhood I was a minor character in a play I didn't understand. The tragedies of those years were yet to have an effect, though I know now that the repercussions of war live long after the battle is done.

I was almost ready that night to go back to my hotel and then take an early morning ferry home to Vancouver Island, when she sat up, stared at me and said, *We are the harbingers of death.* I looked into her crazed eyes, unable to speak, and she fell back upon her pillow. *What do you mean?* I said. She turned her head, a few wisps of hair falling across her cheek, and gave me an odd, childlike smile.

Remember? Nineteen fourteen, and nineteen thirty-nine.

The first years of the great wars of her century. We had both been born at the beginning of a world war, hers the first and mine the second. The words were not her last to me, but they were her last words that night. Her eyes finally closed. I pulled the blanket up and tucked it in around her. At the foot of the bed across from my mother rested the ward cat, a small animal whose spiritual presence gave solace to the sick and dying. The cat was a gift to those who were passing back into the wild. It rested upon the bed of a woman who had been in a coma for a long time. As I left I said goodbye to my mother and to the other women, who slept on. I ran my hand over the cat's grey back. She raised her head to me and purred.

Good night, little one, I said. *Good night.*

I OFFER THESE BRIEF ANECDOTES of my mother and me as a way of coming close to the idea of memory and how it lives on in us, a kind of alternate life, a shadow world of experience, fictions made from fragments of the past, our fears and frailties, our wishes and dreams. History is a story we have told ourselves so often we finally believe it. The wise teachers of this world tell us we must let old memories go, that dwelling upon the past is to deny the present. They say the world, both physical and spiritual, is always in the now, and I agree. Yet I wonder at denying the years that precede us, for surely we are the sum of all we have experienced. To visit lost years, however dangerous it might be, can help relieve the pain of the past. When we do look, we see but dimly. Life is full of dark doors; only by opening them can we let in the light. Forgiveness can be found in such illumination, not only forgiveness of others but of ourselves. Such visits do not always provide us with the healing of past injuries, but memory can offer insights into our lives and those we shared them with. I know my mother today not only by what I remember but by *how* I remember her. She is a story made from intricate details, bits and pieces of what I knew of her long life. My mother's outcry, her telling me that she and I were *harbingers of death*, was not meant as some doom-ridden prophecy but rather an acknowledgment of a bond we shared. We were the children of wars, and those wars had defined us. She told me to remember them, and I have.

ON A SPRING DAY IN MAY in 1915, during a lull in the Second Battle of Ypres, Major John McCrae, a field surgeon, sat in the lee of an ambulance and finished writing the poem "In Flanders Fields" to commemorate the death of his friend Alexis Helmer, who had been blown to pieces by an exploding artillery shell the day before. As McCrae wrote his poem, around him in the desolation created by the war, wild poppies, scrub flowers whose scattered seed is both tenacious and prolific, had grown on the broken land and were, on that May day, in bloom. Their fragile beauty in the midst of the carnage, their resemblance to blots of blood flung to the wind and splattered across the battleground, and their association with the numbing relief of opium and morphine, spoke of the war to him and so became the presiding image in his poem.

What parts of Helmer's body they could salvage were gathered together and placed inside a couple of small sandbags, wrapped in an army blanket and buried nearby. His grave, like so many others after the war, was never found, obliterated in the unrelenting conflict that would go on for another three and a half years. That spring, the larks sang as they always had, the males rising high above no man's land in the hope of attracting a mate while below them the nests where the females huddled were destroyed by the bombardments. No nestlings were born in no man's land, but the hopeful larks still sang.

The casualties in the First World War numbered thirty-seven million. A generation later, a short twenty-seven years, the Second World War casualties were estimated at sixty to eighty million. That estimates of the number of dead and injured could vary by up to twenty million says much about the carnage from 1939 to 1945.

When I revisit McCrae's poem I find in its rhetorical flourishes a pathos close to the sentimental. Surely no soldier stumbling back to the lines across no man's land dragging a friend's corpse behind him in the massacre at Ypres would understand the sentiments of "To you from failing hands we throw / the torch; be yours to hold it high." No matter my sympathy with McCrae's need to create something beautiful out of his friend's death, my discomfort remains. Helmer's body was reduced to bits and pieces of what was once a man: here a piece of his shoulder with the skin still attached to muscle and bone, there a hand without its fingers, part of a knee, an ear, a heart. The doctor had seen death in all its terrible details. He had worked in a field hospital and seen the bodies of men reduced to almost nothing. He had sawed off their arms and legs, pushed a lung back into a shattered chest, had bound a skull, knitting the bones together with wire. His poem tried to find something honourable in Helmer's demise, and why should I question him? John McCrae wanted his friend's rude death to be seen as a noble sacrifice.

The Second Battle of Ypres, in which Alexis Helmer died, claimed six thousand Canadian and sixty thousand British lives. The Germans suffered a loss of thirty-five thousand. The Somme was only a year away. That battle saw the slaughter of a million men in three months, troops from both sides being sent again and again by their generals into the chattering maw of the machine guns. The bodies of thousands were buried in pits, the flesh, bones and organs mixed together, all hearts the same in the anonymity of blood.

"In Flanders Fields" appeared in *Punch* magazine in December 1915 and soon became the most popular poem of the war, especially in America. But what happens when we place McCrae's poem beside those of other war poets, the works of Siegfried Sassoon, Rupert Brooke, Robert Graves or Wilfred Owen? When we compare "In Flanders Fields" to Wilfred Owen's "Anthem for Doomed Youth," what do we feel? Owen's poem speaks of the deaths of young men like Alexis Helmer, but it's unlikely to be read at the cenotaph on Remembrance Day. Were that to happen, there might be fewer tears and greater anger at the wreckage of small hamlets and great cities, the waste of lives in the trenches of France and in the kitchens of homes where lonely women placed their faces in cupped hands to hide their grief from the children who played at their feet.

What passing-bells for these who die as cattle?
   – Only the monstrous anger of the guns.
   Only the stuttering rifles' rapid rattle
Can patter out their hasty orisons.
No mockeries now for them; no prayers nor bells;
   Nor any voice of mourning save the choirs,–

The shrill, demented choirs of wailing shells;
And bugles calling for them from sad shires.

What candles may be held to speed them all?
Not in the hands of boys, but in their eyes
Shall shine the holy glimmers of goodbyes.
The pallor of girls' brows shall be their pall;
Their flowers the tenderness of patient minds,
And each slow dusk a drawing-down of blinds.

IN 1951, the second year of the Korean War, I was twelve years old. I sat beside my grandfather in the living room of a home that was built for veterans. He told me that if the conflict lasted long enough I could go over there to fight. I remember feeling awed by him including me in the idea of war. As he talked, he was drawing from memory a map of the trenches at Ypres, where he fought. He told me of the day he saw chlorine gas rolling like ground fog toward their line. He said it smelled like pineapple and pepper. *I knew death was coming to get me*, he said. When he and some of his fellow soldiers fled, an officer tried to shoot him in the back. The officer was dead from the gas when my grandfather returned to the line. He told me he was surprised he wasn't executed by one of the firing squads. He went on to fight another two years in the hell of no man's land, his survival in that murderous war a miracle.

Each November, I think of my mother's bedridden cry: *We are the harbingers of death.*

I wonder now if she spoke not only of the curiosity of our birth dates falling in the years the two wars began but of humanity and the changes it rings as conflict follows conflict in one inexorable line through the centuries. The list is long.

I look back, and in each of my seventy-five years there has been a war. They are not simply the story of battles, of defeats and victories. The victims are not just soldiers and civilians killed or injured in combat but also a vast number of ordinary people, the ones left standing alone when the wars end. The wives and husbands, the lovers and friends, the children of the dead and injured, they are also who remain when the conflict passes, be it in Korea, Vietnam, Tibet, Chechnya or Afghanistan.

MY FATHER SERVED in the army from 1939 to 1945. We lived in Nelson then, and wouldn't move to the Okanagan Valley until after the war. He came home a few times after guarding the Welland Canal in Ontario and before embarking for England in 1941. I was not quite three years old on his last visit before he left for Europe. My single memory is the day of his leaving and the small bag of oranges my mother gave him to eat on the train. She refused to go down to the station and see him off. She could barely contain her anger whenever she spoke of him joining the army, at thirty years old, leaving behind a wife and three children to survive on a soldier's pay. He had another reason not to enlist: the silicosis he got from working in the hard-rock mines of the Kootenays. His lungs were weak from the quartz crystals he'd breathed in daily for years. The scar tissue whispered every word he spoke, his conversations full of sighs.

On that last visit he carried me to the end of the boardwalk below our house where the trail led down the mountain to the train station in Nelson. It is my earliest memory. The mustiness of his uniform has stayed with me for seventy-three years. The odour of damp wool today undoes me, the smell casting me back into my father's arms. My two older brothers were running alongside him. The three of us were told we could go with him only to the trail head. We were not to go down the mountain. At the end of the boardwalk the bag of oranges broke and they rolled down the path in front of us. I watched my brothers run ahead to gather them up. The golden fruit looked like bright jewels in the litter of dust and crushed leaves. I struggled to get down and join my brothers, but instead of letting me go my father lifted me in his great hands and, laughing, threw me into the sky.

I don't remember coming down.

IN THE EARLY SPRING of 1946 a stranger came into our lives, a kind of hero, a soldier back from the war. He both frightened and thrilled my brothers and me. Our mother told us we had a father again. We were shy of him, but at the same time we were overwhelmed by our fierce desire that he love us, that we love him. He hadn't lived with us for a long time, and we were strangers to him too. The night of his return I woke in my mother's bedroom on a small mattress on the floor below the window looking out over Kootenay Lake. I had slept with her in the big bed all the years my father had been away, my two older brothers sharing a room across the hall. But I didn't sleep in the big bed anymore. What I woke to was the sound of my mother crying out. I sat up and saw a dark shape on top of her. I heard her cries and what I know now were the groans of my father. I stood on my mattress and looked out the window, down at the white-capped waves of the lake and the mountain ranges of the Purcells and Selkirks rising above them. I left my body then. I flew out over the trees and into the sky above Kootenay Lake, the dark waters below me with their stutters of foam and the night sky above riddled with stars. I wasn't afraid of what I had seen and heard. What I felt was a profound loneliness that has never gone away.

AFTER THE REMEMBRANCE DAY ceremony we walk down the alley behind the house and turn in the gate, three crows lifting from the cottonwood in the back yard and cawing at us. *That's a murder of crows,* my mother says. I ask her why she calls them that, and she says, *Because there aren't any larks around here.*

We sit in the kitchen and eat soup together, my brothers somewhere playing with their friends. When we finish she sends me out to do my chores.

An hour later the wood is piled up in the shed, the kindling split and stacked by the door. I put the hatchet away like my father showed me and close the shed door. I walk to the butchers on Main Street with a list and bring back a small piece of chuck steak and some liver and kidneys for the pie my mother is going to make for my father to eat when he comes home from the Legion. When I bring the package home, blood from the organs has seeped from the brown butcher paper and stained the front of my coat. My mother scolds me as she pulls my coat off and drapes it over the board counter by the sink. She pours cold soapy water on the stain and begins to scrub it. As she does, the bloody water drips on the floor. It is when I ask her about the larks, what kind of birds they are, that my mother starts crying. She scrubs at the blood even harder and then stops, her hand shaking.

Oh, hell, she says. *Oh, hell.*

I have never heard my mother swear, never seen her cry. It frightens me. I touch her hand and she draws it away.

I draw my pictures and colour them for a while, but the morning at the cenotaph bothers me. I keep thinking of the poppy my mother threw away. I leave the house and spend the next two hours up on the hill behind the creek. It is where I always go when I am lonely. I sit in a shallow bowl of stone on the lip of the cliff and stare out across the last houses and past the far cupola of the Ukrainian church to the scree at the foot of the broken hills and the pale blue mountains beyond.

There is still enough light for me to find the blossom that lies at the cenotaph among the trodden bootprints of the veterans.

I CROSS THE OPEN GROUND and pass over the shining prints in the ice that mark the places where the soldiers have been, where my father stood. I look at the tracks the old men from the other wars have left, Mr. Jones from the Boer War, and old Mr. Acuff from the Civil War, whose white beard goes all the way down to his belt. My mother has told me Mr. Acuff is the oldest soldier there ever was. I see the small prints of my gumboots beside my mother's narrow shoeprints.

I stand in the snow and ice at the cenotaph, saying to myself over and over the words from the poem she read to me that morning.

We are the Dead.

We are the Dead.

I say it over and over.

The dark comes on, the broken shoulders of the hills in the west gathering long shadows among the scars of the coulees. A weak and falling sun brushes the far mountains. The earth beyond the clouds drags the day away. The poppy is there where she'd been standing. I pick it up and brush the ice crystals away. The flower melts in my hand, the pin shining through it like a thin stripe of light. I fold the poppy in my fist and feel the pin stick into my palm. The pain feels good. I try to find a word for it, but there is no word in me for what I feel.

Not yet.

The pillar of names lies on the snow before me, its shadow a heavy blade under the thin moon. As I walk away I think about what it would be like to *break faith* with people who die. I am pretty sure I know what the poem means and I know I would never do that. I cross the street and follow the long alley down toward the creek and home, back to the place where my mother is. There are no lights in the alley, but I know the way. The poppy is still in my fist.

At the gate I lift my face into the dark. *No one is going to die,* I say. *Not ever.* I wait a moment, then close the gate and cross the yard. I look through the window at my mother in the kitchen. She is leaning over the stove, feeding a stick of wood into the fire. A flame licks around her wrist. She turns, but I know she can't see me. I open the door, and when my mother comes over I hold out my hand. She stands there and I think, by the way she is looking, she might not want the poppy. Then she takes it. I kick off my gumboots and hang my coat on the nail by the back door.

I kneel on the wooden chair and she sits by my side. My brown paper is spread out on the table, the tanks I drew in the afternoon waiting for me. My Mason jar is there too, full of crayons. I pick up a red one and begin.

My father is at the Legion with the other soldiers.

We will sit here at the table, I think. The two of us will sit together. We won't talk. We won't say anything. We will sit here together and wait for my father to come home.

The cenotaph, Whitehall, London, 2014.

MARY JANIGAN
TREASON TO THEIR MEMORY

IT WAS THE MOST DIVISIVE and regrettable election campaign in Canadian history. The year was 1917. On one side was Sir Robert Borden's Union government, which gathered his Conservatives and many English-Canadian dissenters from the Liberal Party into an uneasy coalition. Those partisans called for national unity—under themselves—and conscription to reinforce the troops in the trenches. On the other side were Sir Wilfrid Laurier and his alliance of nationalist francophone Quebecers and a loyal remnant of anglophone Liberals. Laurier vowed to suspend the enforcement of conscription until he could hold a referendum on the issue. Their war of terrible words throughout the autumn of 1917 conveniently coincided with a Victory Bond drive that urged Canadians to make sacrifices for the safety of the "The Boys." And throughout both campaigns, the words and images of "In Flanders Fields" coiled with powerful effect.

The poem had a formidable power among English Canadians to evoke memory and loss. Less than two years after its first publication, it had already inspired many young men to enlist to avenge "the Dead." But that power also intensified the near-catastrophic collision between Quebec and anglophone Canada during the federal election campaign: it fired up the Unionists, who used it to insult Quebecers. After the acrimonious

Shameless and shameful: Unionist election poster, 1917.

mid-year debates over voter eligibility and conscription, Prime Minister Borden wanted to remain publicly aloof from his party's fierce attacks on the Laurier Liberals and aspired to "a truer understanding and comprehension between the various communities."[1] But on November 11, on the eve of his campaign kick-off in Halifax, he handed out an eight-page manifesto that epitomized the conflict ahead.[2]

The prime minister called for "a common patriotism," pleading for "reticence" in handling "old racial and religious quarrels and contentions." That was followed by his definition of patriotism, spelled out in capital letters:

THOSE WHO GAVE THEIR LIVES FOR US ON THE
FAR-AWAY FIELDS OF BATTLE CHERISHED THE VISION
OF A UNITED CANADA. TO DENY THE VISION WOULD
BE TREASON TO THEIR MEMORY

That charge of "treason" set the tone for the December 17 election battle. Borden launched his campaign on the same day as the opening of the three-week Victory Bond drive. He promised to win the war through conscription—and to honour the memory of the fallen. The Unionist and the bond campaigns both marshalled such heady words as *loyalty, patriotism, unity, sacrifice, blood and atrocity*, in posters, advertisements, speeches, flyers and pamphlets. And both campaigns, explicitly and implicitly, evoked "In Flanders Fields," with its poppies, its torch and its terrible message from the Dead.

Laurier and his Liberals were always *les autres*, "the others," unpatriotic regional and cultural outliers who opposed Borden's united government and, in an act of treason against the Dead, denied Borden's vision. In Unionist publicity, Sir Wilfrid and his supporters, including *Le Devoir* editor and former MP Henri Bourassa, appeared almost as threatening as the German Kaiser. And Borden, who played politics with weary resignation and able henchmen, never publicly showed distaste for his government's vicious campaign. In fact, he clearly approved. In his diary, he recorded meetings throughout the campaign with key advisors on organization and publicity. He reviewed at least one anti-Quebec pamphlet with his inner circle. Privy Council president Newton Rowell thought the anti-Quebec rhetoric "might be toned down with advantage." Thomas White, the finance minister, called for "a strong campaign against Quebec."[3] Both ministers agreed: "We should attack in press and on public platform the attitude of Quebec."[4] The prime minister was complicit. He believed that he had a duty to win for the sake of the soldiers.

No one could fail to get the message—especially when Britain supported the messengers. Britain provided a free Imperial news service to Canada, while the Borden government subsidized the Canadian Press. The imagined community of English Canada heeded those calls. They bought bonds in record numbers, purchasing the vast majority of the astonishing $400 million that was raised before the Victory Loan campaign ended on December 1, 1917. Then the Citizens' Unionist Committee, which was composed of prominent government supporters, ran inflammatory advertisements about the fate of that cash if Laurier won.

Patriotic fervour ran high. A pro-Union speaker at the Toronto Women's Liberal Association urged the members to do what they could "for the living at the front and for those who lie beneath alien soil." The Toronto *Globe* reported that the speaker concluded with the "beautiful" poem "In Flanders Fields."[5]

The Unionist publicity committee proclaimed that a lifelong Liberal, E.T. Malone, was switching his support to the Unionists because his younger son was now "buried on the battlefield of Flanders." In that press release, which the *Globe* ran verbatim, Malone said he could not ignore "the call of the dead." Then he cited the last six lines of "In Flanders Fields."[6] Laurier did not have a chance.

British Canadians, as they were then called, voted for Borden's government in droves, handing 153 seats to the Unionists and leaving Laurier's Liberals with 82, including 62 of the 65 seats in Quebec. More than 90 per cent of the military vote went to Borden. In France, the author of "In Flanders Fields," Lieutenant-Colonel John McCrae, took grim satisfaction in voting for the Union government, even though he disliked most politicians. "I hope I stabbed a Fr. Canadian with my vote," he wrote, adding that Quebec nationalist Henri Bourassa "ought to be in prison or dead at the hands of the law."[7]

HOW HAD THIS HAPPENED? How had an achingly poignant poem intensified a rift in the nation's soul, splitting Canadians along linguistic, religious, ethnic and political lines? The passage of a century has obscured how the poem actually affected the war effort and English Canadians. The times were fervid. "In Flanders Fields" became "the poem of the army," and the soldiers "learned it with their hearts."[8] Their younger brothers heard its call to heroism and flocked to enlist.[9] At home, families rationed their food and fuel, bundled together packages for The Boys at the front and watched fearfully for the telegram that would announce a loved one's death. McCrae's friend Sir Andrew Macphail claimed that no recent verse was "more widely known in the civilian world."[10] In 1916, in the foreword to a collection of Great War poems, Susan E. Cameron, assistant warden at Montreal's Royal Victoria College, caught the zeitgeist:

> Gorgeous tragedy with sceptred pall has come sweeping by once more, through a world which was becoming forgetful of her power, and into her train she has swept us all. . . . That bitter sentence, "never to return," is so branded into the consciousness of many of us to-day that it is difficult to see beyond it. . . . With undying pride the country must now cherish the memory of that shining army of youths who will never be old, who at the call of a cause and under the ancient banners of their race, "poured out the red sweet wine of youth; gave up the years to be of hope and joy."[11]

Cameron concluded with the assertion that the task of those fallen soldiers "is still unfinished, and others must follow where they have led."[12] Then she cited the last six lines of "In Flanders Fields," which was included in its entirety in the anthology. In mid-war, the poem was an elegy *and* a fierce promotion for recruitment. The language—so familiar to its listeners from nineteenth-century poets and Bible-based sermons—was a call to remember and a call to arms.

By the spring of 1917, however, after three terrible winters in the trenches, the allure of honour and duty was dimming. Day after day, Canadian newspapers carried lists of the Killed, Missing, Ill and Wounded. Even the heavily censored newspaper reports from the front—with their maps and arrows and their often exaggerated reports of victory—hinted at the stalemate. Men were no longer inundating the recruitment offices, if only because many of those who remained in Canada were needed at home. The Canadian munitions industry was turning out high explosives, airplanes and steel hulls for ships. More than 250,000 workers were producing 100,000 shells each day. The Imperial Munitions Board was at the time the biggest enterprise ever in Canada.[13] The agricultural lobby was also deeply concerned: farmers feared that they would lose their sons and farmhands when they were needed to bring in the crops. Yet English Canada retained an almost unshakeable loyalty to the Mother Country. The voice of the Dead could still touch a deep patriotic impulse among the living; as McCrae's biographer John F. Prescott recounts, McCrae's poem was used "for recruiting, raising money, attacking both pacifists and profiteers, and comforting the relatives of the dead."[14] But the number of new recruits could not keep up with the number of casualties.

In the early years of the war, Prime Minister Borden had always avoided any talk of conscription. In January 1916, he had even assured Parliament that he had no intention of imposing it. By December 1916, however, with conditions at the front worsening, he had flatly refused to reassure labour leaders that he would never invoke conscription—although he had repeated his call for voluntary enlistment.[15]

In early February 1917, the prime minister went to Britain for sessions of the Imperial War Cabinet, and on the Continent he saw the grim war conditions first-hand. In mid-March, he visited injured soldiers in British hospitals, including the No. 3 Canadian General Hospital in Dannes-Camiers, near Boulogne, where medical director John McCrae guided him. (McCrae wearily observed that this was "a form of duty which makes me very tired.")[16] Borden also went up Mont-Saint-Éloi for "a good view of the fighting area."[17] Then he travelled across what had been no man's land to the town of Albert. "Throughout our stay," he would write in his memoirs, "heavy guns were thundering and shells bursting."[18] A month later, after four days of brutal fighting, Canadian troops captured Vimy Ridge, an escarpment northeast of Arras. More than 3,500 Canadians died and more than 7,000 were injured. But voluntary enlistment in April had secured fewer than 5,000 men.

Borden's trip intensified his concern about this trend. Four days after he returned home, on May 18, 1917, he told Parliament that he would propose conscription to secure reinforcements "to maintain the Canadian army in the field. . . . The number of men required will not be less than 50,000, and will probably be 100,000."[19] The House of Commons erupted. Farmers and labour leaders objected to the loss of manpower on the domestic front, and francophone Roman Catholic Quebecers protested their forced inclusion in what they viewed as Britain's war.

The private political bargaining was as fierce as the public debate. In late May, Borden asked Liberal leader Laurier to join him in a coalition government as his deputy. On June 6, Laurier refused. On June 11, Borden introduced the Military Service Act to conscript male citizens between the ages of twenty and forty-four for the duration of the war. The prime minister was also quietly recruiting a Union government that would include dissident Liberals who supported conscription. To avoid an election, he even offered to resign in favour of a leader who would be more palatable to the Liberals. But on August 9, Laurier insisted that Borden face the voters; the last election had been in 1911, and Borden could no longer use the crisis of wartime to postpone a reckoning. By August 25, the prime minister was, as he wrote in his diary, "almost on [the] verge of collapse. Trying starvation and rest cure."[20] On August 29, the

Military Service Act became law, and it would be enforced from January 1, 1918.

Meanwhile, Borden's government was busily sweetening its electoral chances. In mid-August, it introduced the Military Voters Act, which extended the vote to all soldiers, no matter where they were, even if they were underage. In early September, it tabled the War-time Elections Act, which enfranchised roughly one million female relatives of soldiers and disenfranchised anyone of enemy-alien birth who had not been naturalized before March 31, 1902, and who did not have a relative in the military. Many of those roughly fifty thousand disenfranchised residents were Ukrainian-born men who opposed the Austro-Hungarian Empire. Their main sin appeared to be that they usually voted Liberal. By mid-October, Borden had assembled a cabinet that included such prominent anglophone Liberals as former Alberta premier Arthur Sifton. He was ready to face the nation.

The tensions between francophone Quebecers and English Canadians within Quebec and the rest of Canada were already enormous. In 1912, the Ontario Ministry of Education had introduced Regulation 17, which restricted the use of French as a language of instruction to the first two years of elementary school. A year later, Ontario amended the regulation to permit the teaching of French for one hour each day. The Quebec government protested vehemently. Why should it be the only province to endorse bilingual education? The bitter feelings deepened during the war. In March 1916, Manitoba banned all bilingual schools, partly as a backlash against German-language instruction. Along the way, the Manitoba government wiped out French-language instruction, which had existed since the days of the Red River missionary schools.

In Quebec, the caustic reaction against those decisions pitted francophone Roman Catholic Quebecers against anglophone Catholics and Protestants in the province and in the rest of the country, where "In Flanders Fields" was already "quite popular" by the spring of 1916.[21] Laurier supported the war—but he opposed conscription, which he had always dreaded. In early June 1916, he had delivered a fiery recruiting speech in French in Montreal, denouncing those "bitter, warped, prejudiced little souls" who refused to enlist in the "holiest crusade in history." He had added: "Even the Church must not shirk."[22] His appeal had little effect. In September 1916, alarmed by the escalating domestic war of words, Pope Benedict XV intervened, urging all members of the Catholic hierarchy to preach moderation. In November 1917, the Judicial Committee of the British Privy Council, which was then Canada's highest court, declared that the Constitution protected Roman Catholic schools in Ontario but not French-language schools. Recruitment remained an uphill battle in Quebec.

There was another complication: many Quebecers saw little appeal in fighting the wars of Great Britain and France. They felt an attachment to Quebec, and to Canada, but not to imperialist Britain. Their clergy also felt little loyalty to France as the Mother Country. As Prime Minister Borden ruefully mused in his memoirs, they "had been alienated from their natural sympathy by confiscation of religious houses and property and by the growth of atheistic outlook and tendency in France."[23] As well, some Quebecers felt that France had abandoned them generations ago, after the British conquest of French North America.

By the autumn of 1917, as the campaigns for Victory Bonds and for the December 17 election commenced, the mutual suspicions were strong. "In Flanders Fields"—with its evocations of torches and poppies and the Dead who could not sleep—was a pivotal tool in those campaigns. And it was largely used against Liberal leader Laurier and francophone Quebecers. The bond drive, the election campaign, the battles on the Western Front, the themes of "In Flanders Fields" and the insulting references to Sir Wilfrid Laurier's Liberals became inextricably entwined in the weeks leading up to the vote, each reinforcing the other.

The propaganda was intense. On November 15, the Canadian Press reported that the German attack to drive the Canadians off Passchendaele ridge had failed: "The story of Passchendaele is one of severe enemy casualties, steady loss of ground and declining morale. The Canadian corps has moved steadily to its objectives."[24] That was certainly not the whole story. At Passchendaele, or the Third Battles of Ypres, Canada captured a ruined village after a month of battle and more than fifteen thousand casualties, which today "has come to symbolize the horrors of the Western Front . . . a price no Canadian thought worth paying."[25] In 1917, however, the Canadian Press journalist could not resist an uplifting touch. "The achievement has been great. The cost has been heavy. Many noble men of yours have died for Canada."[26] He ended his report with the last three lines of "In Flanders Fields." The Dead would not sleep if the living broke faith and did not enlist.

Press reports like this ensured that "the experience of war as expressed in news coverage reshaped the meaning of nationality."[27] In late 1916, the British government had put the Reuters news agency under direct government control because of its financial problems. In March 1917, it had augmented the agency with a supplementary service of roughly twenty thousand words per month—"to strengthen morale throughout the empire"—that was sent free of charge to the Ottawa bureau of the Canadian Press for cross-Canada distribution.[28] Meanwhile, the Borden government had offered an annual subsidy of $50,000 to Canadian Press to reduce its costs for telegraph transmission to its 117 members. The power of the press to shape Canada's sense of community, particularly among English Canadians, was formidable.

Canadian firms were buying advertisements to support the bond drive virtually every day, often invoking "In Flanders Fields" to rally English Canadians. On November 16, electrical suppliers McDonald & Willson ran a drawing of Lord Nelson at the helm of *Victory* along with the exhortation "Those who fight on the bloody Flanders plains look to us at home to supply them with all the requisites of successful war."[29] A day later, a Mrs. A.W. McDougald of Montreal, "daughter of the late Honorable James Bethune of Toronto," published a pamphlet about women's wartime sacrifices to raise funds for the Imperial Order Daughters of the Empire. The cover showed "white crosses sown thickly on a Flanders field."[30]

At least one bond-drive poster in 1917 reinforced that message. It shows an infantryman in a generic tartan kilt in front of a field of poppies and distant artillery; the slogan reads, "Doing My Bit: Four Years. Do Yours: Buy Victory Bonds."[31] It was not until the 1918 bond campaign, however, after John McCrae's death on January 28, that the posters would unreservedly deploy "In Flanders Fields" with poppy fields and torches and such poignant lines as "Be yours to hold it high!" and "If ye break faith . . . we shall not sleep."[32]

But the burgeoning popularity of the poem was evident in

Overleaf: Frank Lucien Nicolet, "If Ye Break Faith—We Shall Not Sleep", 1918.

"If ye break faith —
we shall not sleep"

BUY VICTO

RY BONDS

the 1917 bond drive, which elicited enormous support from corporate Canada and regular English Canadian voters. Canada's banks sponsored advertisements that offered installment plans for wage earners and small investors who wanted to buy bonds. On November 21, the Julian Sale Leather Goods Company urged the nation to show itself "not unworthy of its sons who have won such imperishable honor on the fields of France and Flanders."[33] Two days later, the minister of militia, S.C. Mewburn, reminded a female audience in Hamilton, Ontario, that an estimated thirty thousand women in that city would be eligible to vote for the first time in a federal election because their male relatives were "with the colors on Flanders fields." To support those men, the women should vote for the Union government.[34] The Sterling Bank of Canada urged the purchase of Victory Bonds with the slogan

THE MAN IN FLANDERS IS ASKED TO SACRIFICE—
YOU ARE ASKED ONLY TO INVEST.[35]

Veterans thronged Borden's rallies, talking about the bullets lodged in their bodies. They were inevitably described as soldiers "who fought and fell on Flanders fields. They have come home with honorable wounds."[36] In one Ontario town, they formed a guard of honour for Borden.

The Unionists could expect little from Quebec, but they had largely conquered English Canada. Many recent immigrants (and Liberal supporters) from Eastern Europe could not vote. To appease the agricultural lobby, the Unionists even promised in late November to exempt farmers' sons who produced food from military service. Laurier could not win.

The rhetoric became more extreme after the bond drive

ended on December 1. In large advertisements, the Unionist publicity committee warned, "The Ballot Is a Weapon in Your Hands: Oppose Union Government Now and You Turn That Weapon on Your Own Soldier Relative or Friend in the Trenches."[37] In a pitch to Ontario residents, the publicity committee explained that Canadians had just subscribed $400 million in bonds "to keep Canada in the war, to reinforce the decimated regiments in France, and to assist in defeating a brutal, arrogant, and merciless foe." The headline read, "Shall Those Who Will Not Fight for Canada Govern Canada?" The text added that if Ontario did not vote for the Union government, "Quebec will exercise a dictatorship over the other Provinces."[38] The publicity committee even put out a pamphlet on German atrocities that could not fail to inflame voters with its tales of the "Fiendish Slaughter of Children" and "most diabolical" treatment of women.[39]

In effect, the Union government appropriated "In Flanders Fields" so completely that voters identified its candidates with the poem. On the brink of the election, one anonymous letter writer, who called himself a "True Canadian," used the poem to denounce the Laurier Liberals. In his imagination, he said, he had wandered in Flanders fields, where the oppressed troops "suffer for YOU." He had seen the soldiers who "fight for YOU." And he had "walked among the crosses beneath which sleep so many of Canada's dauntless sons. . . . They died for YOU."[40] His fury was almost biblical. When a Laurier Liberal candidate warned Methodist ministers to keep out of the campaign, Private Sidney Lambert, "who left a limb on Flanders' fields," hobbled onto a Unionist platform to explain that he was a Methodist preacher who would not heed that advice.[41] He was cheered. Two days before the election, at a meeting of the

Women's Auxiliary of the 10th Battalion, one woman claimed that the rest of Canada would not have contributed so much for Victory Bonds if it thought that "those slackers" in Quebec would be spending it. Her nephew, she added, lay "in Flanders"; her son lay "under the poppies in France"; and her other son was "back with only one leg."[42]

Such language conjured up villains. English Canadians were not just fighting the "Huns," they were fighting their dignified former prime minister Sir Wilfrid Laurier and the prominent Quebec journalist Henri Bourassa, who had only recently switched his support to the Laurier Liberals. A century later, the Unionist pamphlets remain startling. "An Open Letter from A Winnipeg Mother to Sir Wilfrid Laurier," which was reprinted from the *Free Press* for cross-Canada circulation, was a plea from a "mother of the dead" whose two sons "lie in their graves on the battle-scarred field of Flanders." The anonymous woman noted that Laurier had deplored "the raising of racial and other questions" throughout Canada, but, she told Laurier, "you are the One Man in Canada, who, by taking a firm and imperial stand at this time of our national peril, has the power to quell" those slurs.[43] The woman warned that "the blood of the dead heroes in Flanders calls to you," and she threatened "swift and just punishment," presumably at the polls, if he failed to listen.[44] A copy of "In Flanders Fields" was appended to the pamphlet. Under McCrae's name was the pointed notation "Now serving in France."

Another election pamphlet was entitled "English Canadians and the War." It narrowed the election question to this: "Is Canada to stay in the war or quit?" The "oily-tongued followers of Laurier and Bourassa" might claim that their leaders wanted to keep Canada in the war, but, the pamphlet claimed, Laurier's strongest supporters were extremists who had "howled down" Unionist orators in Quebec while "pro-Germans" had drowned out the prime minister. (Armed protestors had disrupted a Borden rally in Kitchener, Ontario, on November 24.) Should Quebec extremists such as Bourassa, "coupled with the Pro-German and slacker element . . . be allowed to rule the country?" Most important, would a Laurier victory "be fair play to the memory of those 35,000 Canadian dead lying in Flanders?"[45]

English Canadians understood the message: Quebecers were untrustworthy citizens who would not let the Dead sleep in Flanders. Quebecers understood the message too: their fellow Canadians were vilifying them—and isolating them. Borden's diary makes frequent references throughout the campaign to the disruption of Unionist rallies in Quebec. "Meetings in Quebec broken up by French agitators," read one entry during the second week of the campaign.[46] The prime minister did not address any rallies in the province. Nor did he record any private qualms about his government's responsibility for the heightened emotions.

The Unionists were relentless. One election leaflet, "Women of Canada and the War Franchise Act," which was endorsed by the presidents of four women's organizations, including the National Council of Women, supported the government's move to extend female suffrage just to women with soldiers in the family through the War-time Elections Act. Those women who could vote would "remain true to [Canada's] sacred trust to the Canadian men now fighting the battle of freedom."[47] Few English Canadians would miss the allusions to McCrae's injunction to hold high the torch. In another pamphlet, Scottish Canadians were told that they could not continue to support Laurier when "those brave men in Flanders" needed reinforcement: "Too many young men from Canada once showing in frank open faces their Scottish ancestry lie beneath 'where poppies blow in Flanders' fields.'" The pamphlet ended by equating a vote for the Quebec Liberals of Henri Bourassa with the deserters in a poem from Robert Burns: "Wha will be a traitor knave? Wha can fill a coward's grave?"[48] Yet another pamphlet maintained that "the failure of Laurier to rally his race in the war" had created "a wave of race bigotry and desire for French-Canadian domination." Only the Union government could control "a situation pregnant with peril."[49]

An election poster, showing Laurier in a toga with a wreath around his head, read, "The Fiddler: Nero 'Fiddling' with Politics while the Flames Spread. Vote Union Government."[50] Another, showing two Canadian soldiers manning a machine gun, read, "Keep It in Action: Every Union Ballot Is a Bullet for the Kaiser. Vote Union Government."[51] A third showed the Kaiser as "One Who Is Pleased" in front of "Laurier's Policy Manifesto," which read, "Desert and Betray Canada's Boys at the Front," and was endorsed by Henri Bourassa with an "O.K." and his signature at the bottom.[52] It was shameless—and shameful.

"IN FLANDERS FIELDS" might have reinforced the Western Front with patriots, but it also reinforced Canada's two solitudes. The sons of English Canadians enlisted, fired with the desire to take the torch from failing hands. Their fathers and mothers, their friends and relatives, subscribed to war bonds and believed Union government allegations that francophone Quebecers were traitors. Support for Laurier and opposition to conscription was betrayal of the Dead, who would not sleep beneath their blankets of poppies. The wartime election of 1917 wreaked huge damage among the federation partners as the Union government targeted the Laurier Liberals with almost as much ferocity as it aimed at the Huns. It is remarkable that Canada remained intact. And "In Flanders Fields"—with its haunting evocations of lost lives and its fierce call to arms—provided the ammunition that Canadians would deploy against their fellow Canadians.

NOTES

1. "War Policy and Problems To Be Union Govt's First Duty," *The Toronto Daily Star*, Friday, October 19, 1917, p. 17.

2. "Manifesto of Sir Robert Borden to the Canadian People," Union Government Publicity Bureau, 1917, p. 8. University of Toronto Libraries, Canadian Pamphlets and Broadsides Collection.

3. Diary of Sir Robert Borden (transcript), Sunday, November 25, 1917. Library and Archives Canada, MG26H, vol. 450, p. 278.

4. Diary of Sir Robert Borden (transcript), Monday, November 26, 1917. Library and Archives Canada, MG26H, vol. 450, p. 278.

5. "Take No Side in Election," *Globe*, Friday, November 30, 1917, p. 10.

6. "Supports Union for Sake of Boys," *Globe*, Friday, November 30, 1917, p. 9.

7. John F. Prescott, *In Flanders Fields: The Story of John McCrae* (Guelph: Guelph Historical Society, 2003), p. 125. Prescott provided no footnotes for these quotes, although they were almost certainly from McCrae's letters to his mother.

8. Andrew Macphail, "An Essay in Character," in John McCrae, *In Flanders Fields and Other Poems* (Toronto: William Briggs, 1919), p. 57.

9. As McCrae's biographer, John F. Prescott notes there were other reasons to enlist, especially in Britain: the sinking of the passenger liner *Lusitania*, Zeppelin raids over England, the use of poison gas and stories of German atrocities. Prescott, p. 105.

10. Macphail, p. 57.

11. Susan E. Cameron, foreword to *In the Day of Battle: Poems of the Great War*, ed. Carrie Ellen Holman (Toronto: William Briggs, 1916), pp. 7–8.

12. Cameron, p. 8.

13. Michael Bliss, *A Canadian Millionaire: The Life and Business Times of Sir Joseph Flavelle, Bart., 1858–1939* (Toronto: Macmillan Company of Canada, 1978), p. ix.

14. Prescott, p. 106.

15. Martin Robin, "Registration, Conscription, and Independent Labour Politics, 1916–1917," in *Conscription 1917* (Toronto: University of Toronto Press, Canadian Historical Readings, vol. 8, 2010), p. 63.

16. Prescott, p. 120.

17. *Robert Laird Borden: His Memoirs*, ed. Henry Borden (Toronto: Macmillan Company of Canada, 1938), p. 687.

18. Ibid., p. 688.

19. Ibid., p. 699.

20. Ibid., p. 735.

21. Linda Sutherland, "The Man Behind the Poppies," in *The McGill News*, November 2013. Sutherland attributes the words to a May 31, 1916, letter from John McCrae to his friend Carlton Noyes, which is stored in the Osler Library of the History of Medicine, http://publications.mcgill.ca/mcgillnews/2013/11/06/the-man-behind-the-poppies.

22. "Sir Wilfrid's Burning Appeal to Compatriots," *Globe*, Monday, June 5, 1916, p. 1.

23. *Robert Laird Borden: His Memoirs*, ed. Henry Borden. (Toronto: Macmillan Company of Canada, 1938), p. 613.

24. W.A. Willison of the Canadian Press, "Huns Cannot Oust Canadians: Currie's Men More Secure Than Ever," *Globe*, Thursday, November 15, 1917, p. 1.

25. Terry Copp, "The Military Effort," in *Canada and the First World War: Essays in Honour of Robert Craig Brown*, ed. David MacKenzie (Toronto: University of Toronto Press, 2005), p. 54.

26. Willison, p. 5.

27. Gene Allen, *Making National News: A History of Canadian Press* (Toronto: University of Toronto Press, 2013), p. 180.

28. Ibid., p. 45.

29. "Victory Bonds and the 'Victory's' Message," *The Toronto Daily Star*, Friday, November 16, 1917, p. 14.

30. "Women's Price for Freedom," *Globe*, Saturday, November 17, 1917, p. 10.

31. Choko, pp. 92–93, and United States Library of Congress Prints & Photographs Online Catalog, http://www.loc.gov/pictures/item/2004666238/.

32. Marc H. Choko, *Canadian War Posters: 1914–1918, 1939–1945* (Ottawa: Canada Communication Group, 1994), pp. 116–17, and Maurice F.V. Doll, *The Poster War: Allied Propaganda Art of the First World War* (Edmonton: Alberta Community Development, 1993), pp. 64–65.

33. "Buy Canada Victory Bonds," *Globe*, Wednesday, November 21, 1917, p. 8.

34. "Reinforcements Needed at Once," *Globe*, Friday, November 23, 1917, p. 1.

35. "Canada Calls," *Globe*, Saturday November 24, 1917, p. 11.

36. "Veterans Back Cause of Union," *Globe*, Thursday, November 29, 1917, p. 1.

37. "Referendum Would Leave Our Fighters in the Lurch!" *The Toronto Daily Star*, Tuesday, December 4, 1917, p. 12.

38. "Shall Those Who Will Not Fight for Canada Govern Canada?" *The Toronto Daily Star*, Wednesday, December 5, 1917, p. 13.

39. *"German Atrocities,"* Union Government Publicity Bureau. Library and Archives Canada, MicF, CC-4-84424, no. 33286500694316, pp. 2–3.

40. "Is This Your Letter?" *Globe*, Tuesday, December 11, 1917, p. 1.

41. "Ramsden Gets Direct Answer," *Globe*, Thursday, December 13, 1917, p. 8.

42. "If Mistake Is Made Monday," *Globe*, Saturday, December 15, 1917, p. 10.

43. "An Open Letter from a Winnipeg Mother to Sir Wilfrid Laurier," reprinted from the Winnipeg *Free Press* of August 14, 1917 (Ottawa: Union Government Publicity Bureau, 1917). Library and Archives Canada, AC901, A7, 1917, no. 0055-019100150002 B04-TR2001 982968, p. 2.

44. Ibid.

45. "English Canadians and the War" (Ottawa: Union Government Publicity Bureau, 1917). Library and Archives Canada, AC901, A7, 1917, (34) C2, Ma-0056, pp. 2, 3, 4.

46. Diary of Sir Robert Borden (transcript), Friday, November 23, 1917. Library and Archives Canada, MG26H, vol. 450, p. 278.

47. "Women of Canada and the War Franchise Act" (Ottawa: Union Government Publicity Bureau, 1917). Library and Archives Canada, AC901, A7, 1917, p. 1.

48. "Scotch Canadians and the War: Can No Longer Follow Sir Wilfrid Laurier" (Ottawa, Union Government Publicity Bureau, n.d.). Library and Archives Canada, AC901, A7, 1917, no. 0053, 01-0334-0007-AO2 TR-2002052946, pp. 2,4.

49. "Plain Facts for English-Speaking Electors: Facts Which Should Be Digested and Taken Seriously to Heart." (Ottawa: Union Government Publicity Bureau, 1917). Library and Archives Canada, MicF, CC-4-84320, no. 33286500694183, p. 7.

50. http://data2.archives.ca/e/e428/e010697147-v8.jpg.

51. http://data2.archives.ca/e/e428/e010697149-v8.jpg.

52. http://data2.archives.ca/e/e350/e008748929-v8.jpg.

NOS BRAS LASSES VOUS TENDENT LE FLAMBEAU. A VOUS, TOUJOURS, DE LE PORTER BIEN

"TO Y...TH FAILING HANDS...THROW THE TORCH. BE YOURS TO HOLD IT

KEN DRYDEN
THE TORCH

OCTOBER 16, 2014—HOME OPENING GAME I was waiting in a corridor near the Montreal Canadiens' dressing room, behind the doors that led to the ice. I was handed a torch, the torch was lighted, the doors opened. I walked forward. The arena was black. On the giant video board, twenty-one thousand fans saw the torch first, then they saw me. The air exploded with noise. At moments like this, I think, *Don't trip*. At this moment, I thought, *Don't set yourself on fire*.

SEPTEMBER 1970—TRAINING CAMP It is almost my first memory of the Canadiens' dressing room. The room was so bright. The white concrete-block walls, the red-and-blue trim, everything painted to a high gloss, glimmering like new under the fluorescent lights. The double row of wood plaques in deep, rich brown that ran above our heads as we put on our gear, one plaque for each season from 1918 onward, and on them, in gold letters, the name of every Canadiens player. Above the plaques, side by side in a line, black-and-white head-shots of former team members who'd been inducted into the Hockey Hall of Fame—Howie Morenz, Georges Vézina, Aurèle Joliat, Bill Durnan, Maurice (the Rocket) Richard, Doug Harvey and many more. And above them was a message like no other in sports.

Be yours to hold it high: Canadiens captain Jean Béliveau in the Montreal dressing room, 1971.

"The price of success is hard work," read the words in the dressing room of the Toronto Maple Leafs. For the Philadelphia Flyers: "You play for the crest on the front, not the name on the back." For the Boston Bruins: "We are what we repeatedly do. Excellence, therefore, is not an act, but a habit." In Pittsburgh, the words of former Penguins coach Bob Johnson: "It's a great day for hockey." In Detroit: "To whom much is given, much is expected."

In Montreal, first in the Forum and now in the Bell Centre, are John McCrae's words from "In Flanders Fields":

To you from failing hands we throw
   The torch; be yours to hold it high.

As a kid in school, I had learned McCrae's poem and recited it every Remembrance Day. I remembered from it the poppies, the crosses, the birds and the guns. I remembered sadness and quiet defiance. I didn't remember the torch.

I didn't know what I was doing there, in that dressing room, in 1970. I was a kid from Etobicoke. These were the *Montreal Canadiens*. They existed on TV. Their players were ten feet tall; they skated a hundred miles an hour. I would get killed or humiliated. Later, when I officially became a member of the team, I never entirely stopped feeling like an imposter. *If these are the real Canadiens*, I thought, *I can't be here. And I am here, so these can't be the real Canadiens.* McCrae's words, in part, defined the reality of this legendary room and the unreality of me being there.

THE STORY OF HOW "In Flanders Fields" came to be in the Canadiens' dressing room begins with Frank Selke Sr., who was named the general manager in 1946. He arrived to a depleted team: the players, almost all anglophone, were aging. The Canadiens had but one great star, Rocket Richard. The Forum's capacity was just 9,300. Selke had two requests of Senator Donat Raymond, the team's owner: rebuild and expand the Forum; and, in a pre-draft era, when teams had to select and develop their own players from a young age, build a farm system across Canada, where all NHL players of the time came from, but most particularly build a farm system in Quebec. Raymond agreed.

By 1952, Selke could see that things were changing. The Forum now seated fourteen thousand. More importantly, his farm system was beginning to bear fruit: Boom Boom Geoffrion, Dickie Moore, Tom Johnson; a year later Jean Béliveau; then Jacques Plante; then Henri Richard and Claude Provost—the team, younger, better and more francophone, was getting ready to win.

Selke had had little formal education, like most young people of his time. He'd begun as an electrician; hockey was his sideline. He also loved to read. In his early twenties, during World War I, he read the poetry of John McCrae, and the themes of "In Flanders Fields" stayed with him. Selke believed in continuity more than transition. You use the past to make the present; you use the present to make the future. Each is a part of the other. Each is necessary to the other. In 1952, it was time to pass the torch to a new generation of the team. He put McCrae's words on the walls of the Canadiens' dressing room.

From 1956 to 1979, in twenty-four years, the Canadiens won the Stanley Cup fifteen times. In the last four years of the 1970s—pre-season, regular season, playoffs—teams I played on, we almost never lost a game of any kind. Again and again, we were asked by journalists from other NHL cities, "What makes you so good? Other teams win sometimes, but nobody wins like you." To say that we had the best players, best coaches and best managers was too obvious. There needed to be something more. Invariably, the journalists would begin their stories with reference to McCrae's words. The Canadiens are *different*, they were saying. This poem, in this place, symbolizes that difference. And their readers, who themselves had never seen anything like it in any dressing room they had been in, understood.

PROFESSIONAL SPORTS TEAMS function in the present and in the near present. As a player, every game, in front of thousands in an arena and hundreds of thousands or more at home, you are on the line. You have a job to do. You have to deliver. They, the fans, are counting on you, and so are your teammates. You are responsible to them; or, in today's more commonly used word, you are "accountable." In the season's opening game ceremony in 2014, after I had passed the torch to Canadiens goalie Carey Price, he passed it to the next player introduced, who passed it to the next one after that. In passing the torch, each player was saying to his teammate, "I trust you." Each recipient was saying, "I accept the responsibility." There, in the spotlight at centre ice, their witnesses were the fans. Player to player, player to fan, player and fan to team, this sealed their bond.

But McCrae's torch, and Selke's torch, is more than that.

Selke put those words in the Canadiens' dressing room, he put them in the mouths of the team's former great players, to help build a tradition. A collective story, with a beginning and a middle but, in this case, no end. With a past, a present *and* a future. Every player who put on a Canadiens jersey, every coach who stepped behind the team's bench, every manager who worked in its offices, had a responsibility, was accountable, to every player, coach and manager who had come before, and to everyone who would come after. That was the bargain. Whether you knew it or not, that's what you had signed up for.

As a player, you know about your team's past, but you are so caught up in meeting the demands of the present, you don't think much about the future. It's towards the end of your career— if you're lucky—and not after it's finished, that it strikes you. Older players helped make you better and make you win; it is now up to you to do the same for those who will continue after.

It is later, too, that players discover that their deepest feelings come from doing something together. We are all selfish. We all want great things for ourselves. I wanted to win individual trophies, to set myself apart from everyone else as a singular star. But then, when we won a Stanley Cup, I discovered just how much better that felt. And I discovered just how much prouder I was to be part of a Canadiens goalie tradition, one that had begun with Vézina, Hainsworth, Durnan and Plante before me, that has extended to Patrick Roy and Carey Price after me, that will continue with others after them.

That's what McCrae was getting at, and what Selke wanted to convey. McCrae's intention was not to commemorate the past and the fallen but to inspire the future. It is one thing, he was saying, for us to fight the fight. But when we pass the torch, as some day we must, if you who receive it don't hold it high, if "ye break faith with us," we shall have died for nothing. We shall have served no purpose and be truly dead.

It is you who come after us that make us matter. It is you who keep us alive.

SHORT DAYS AGO

Above: A reminder that there was life away from the trenches, 1916.

Opposite: Nineteen-year-old Cpl. Eric Heathcote sent this photo
(taken in the winter of 1915–1916) from Belgium to his sweetheart.
He would survive the war and marry the girl.

Above: Tom Longboat, an Onondaga (First Nations) long distance runner and winner of the Boston Marathon in 1907, buys a newpaper from a French paperboy, June 1917.

Opposite: French girls selling fruit and chewing gum. The bags they carry hold gas masks.

Opposite: A Newfoundlander shaves in his trench, Beaumont-Hamel, 1916.

Above: As natural water sources along the Western Front quickly became contaminated, a clean bath required improvisation, rainwater, and a shell hole.

YMCA Captain Robert Pearson umpires a baseball match behind
Canadian lines, September 1917. Concerned about maintaining a soldier's
good health (as well as keeping him out of trouble), the Army, the YMCA
and the Salvation Army often organized sporting events.

Life carries on: *(top)* Voting in the British Columbia provincial elections, location unknown, September 1916; *(above)* picking flowers, July 1917; *(opposite)* fresh blueberries gathered in Bourlon Wood, Arras, France, 1918.

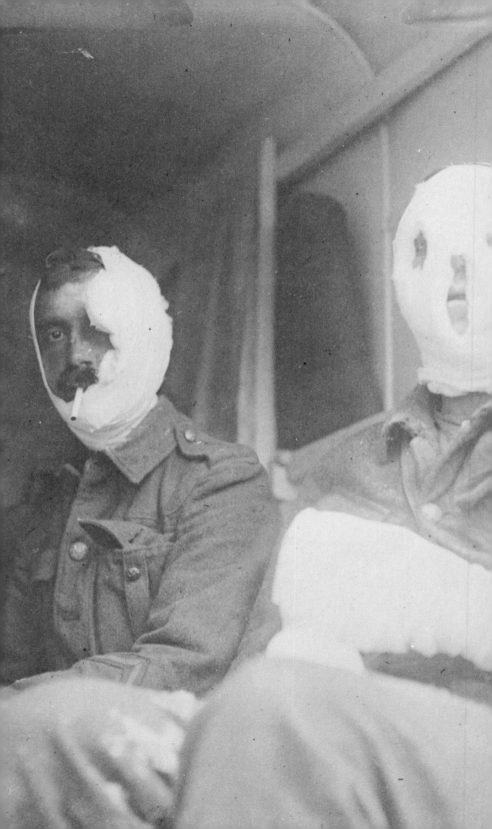

KEVIN PATTERSON
SOLDIER SURGEON, SOLDIER POET

WHEN BATTLE-WOUNDED come to a field hospital, the smell of fresh blood fills the air with a density not known outside an abattoir or a birthing bed: faintly citrus, with deep loamy notes. It is not unpleasant. The hard part of war is not the scent of blood but the associations that the odour carries. The sounds of sobbing and shuddering endure, as do the Dantean sights: shattered bone ripping through skin, viscera spilling out of abdomens like coils of thick pink cable, wide-eyed seventeen-year-old boys exhaling and never again inhaling.

To understand John McCrae's war experience and his poetry, one must imagine carnage on a scale that no one of the information age has seen. The Western Front in World War I, rivalled only by the Eastern in World War II, was industrialized homicide on a scale that resists imagination. The Americans lost 2,400 people in Afghanistan in thirteen years. On July 1, 1916, the first day of the Battle of the Somme, the British Empire took 58,000 casualties, dead and wounded. Sixty miles of prostrate bodies, laid head to toe. In a day.

It was total war, and it consumed every involved nation. McCrae did not go to battle to ease the suffering of its victims. He went to war to help win it, to repair as many of the broken fighters as he could so that they might fight more and break

Wounded Canadians, location unknown, July 1917.

more of the enemy. He wrote that he believed medical personnel were in any event beside the point—what the army needed to win was fighting men. Self-evidently true, this is still surprising to read from the pen of a physician. We are accustomed to doctors considering themselves to be at the very pinnacle of importance in their respective societies; a century later, McCrae's humility is as unexpected as his bellicosity.

McCrae was drawn to battle for the reasons men usually give for loving war: he was stirred by the fellowship of soldiers under arms, and he loved the feeling of waking from sleep that mobilization brings. He had trained as an artillery officer, and upon the outbreak of the Second Boer War in South Africa he volunteered to serve as a gunner. That war saw the invention of the concentration camp. He would not later have been naive about what war is. Through his poetry run paeans to the idea of comradeship and mutual obligation, and from his poetry we learn that these are things he knew best and felt most strongly when in uniform. As veterans are prone to doing, after he came home from the war in South Africa, he missed it.

Throughout his military career, John McCrae considered himself as much a gunner as a medical officer. One of his most painful moments in the Great War, among years of continuous horror, was when he was transferred away from the artillery field hospital and removed from the guns. This is how armies and wars sustain themselves: by giving and drawing from soldiers enough love to obscure the pain they endure and inflict. It's the soulless disconnectedness they experience later, when they come home, that breaks the spell and brings the horrors they saw and committed into focus. Which makes them long for more love, which is to say, more war.

Ten years after the end of the Boer War, on what was by all

accounts an unusually pleasant summer in Western and Central Europe, the love would come back.

THE EYE IS DRAWN to difference, and so our conversations about war emphasize how much combat has changed since McCrae's time. The rise of drones and precision-guided munitions and aeromedical evacuation and satellite imagery has changed some of the decisions generals make. But the essence of McCrae's wars remains the essence of ours: men trying to kill one another with fire. Put some accelerant—nitrates, usually—in with the fuel, and it burns fast. Confine it, and it explodes. Maybe the nitrates come as fertilizer, mixed with diesel fuel and tamped down in a pressure cooker, buried in a road. Maybe carbon is bonded to the nitrates to make gunpowder that pushes a projectile down a tube. To the extent that war has changed, it has changed in these, the engineering details of how shards of metal are blown toward teenagers and whoever else may be standing in the way.

What happens at the other end of those blasts has not changed at all. Bullets tear through intestines in exactly the same way now as they did then. Young people lie in the dirt and feel dread sweep through them as their bowels empty through their abdomen and their hoped-for lives close in and vanish. Lungs fill with blood slowly after a chest shot, and it gets more difficult to breathe until finally it is impossible. When the injury is made by a bullet, it is surprising how quickly such a small hole in someone can kill them. When it's made by a blast, it is surprising how much injury can be survived: limbs entirely avulsed and yet the severed vessels close and clot up, and one way or another the shattered person does not bleed to death, even though the visual evidence is that he must.

McCrae knew the same problems. Hemorrhagic shock, and the pale, sweaty, cold skin that portends it, looked the same to him as it does now. The solution remains, first, blood transfusions, and then a ligature, tied around the bleeding vessel. He had learned how to operate as a medical student, as all medical students did then, when GPs still did appendectomies and hernia repairs. He reacquainted himself with operating after the declaration of war in 1914, when he felt obliged—he thought all unmarried men were—to volunteer for service. He rejoined his beloved artillery by becoming a war surgeon in a field hospital attached to the guns. McCrae had become an infectious-disease consultant at McGill, co-authoring a textbook on pathology. He was no more a trauma surgeon by this point than he was a psychiatrist. But he said he felt duty call him. And he wanted to be back with the guns. The fastest way to do that was to refashion himself as a surgeon. So he became a surgeon. This much is clear: something pulled him hard.

War surgery is first of all about damage control. Not all things that need repair need to be repaired immediately. The battle surgeon's goal is to keep the patient alive long enough to face the deferrable problems. The first priority is to make sure the injured can breathe. Lung-shot men die if they cannot re-inflate their lungs. A tube, connected to suction, placed in the space between the lung and the chest wall accomplishes that goal, and every surgeon who treats penetrating trauma performs this procedure frequently. The next most important thing is to make sure the heart continues beating, and for it to do this effectively it needs blood in the vessels. If the bleeding is happening in one of the extremities, it is usually possible to stop it. A tourniquet placed by a medical assistant in the field may have done this already. Whether amputation can be avoided depends on the size of the wound and the extent of remaining blood supply. Vascular surgery, with its fussy grafting and repairs, was still in its infancy in the early part of the twentieth century, and anyway amputations are among the fastest and easiest operations: given the prospect of having soldiers die while a surgeon works on saving the limb of one of them, the decision to amputate becomes easier as the wagonloads of wounded mount and the surgeon grows more exhausted.

If the patient is bleeding out from a chest wound, it becomes necessary to open the chest, and the hope then is for an easy-to-repair peripheral vessel injury. Hopefully, it will be lacerated but not severed. Hopefully, the great vessels in the midline will not be involved. General surgeons are less happy in the chest than they are in the abdomen—or anywhere else, for that matter, except possibly the head. The farther the wound is out to the side of the chest, the less dangerous it is, and when the rib spreaders open and the midline structures are shown not to be involved, the relief in the room becomes for a moment as pungent as that smell of fresh blood.

If the injured vessel is in the abdomen, different challenges emerge. Viscera have probably been penetrated, and the operative field does not suddenly reveal itself with the puff of a collapsing lung. But in recompense, time moves more slowly in the abdomen. It is easier to clamp the largest vessels without killing the patient, and here there are optional organs; a patient might conceivably survive the removal of a spleen or a kidney or half the liver. This is less true of aortas, hearts and brains.

The ethos of damage-control surgery embraces its own

Overleaf: Canadian and German wounded await triage, 10th Field Ambulance Station, Hangard (Battle of Amiens), France, August 1918.

pragmatism. It confronts both the idea of overwhelming trouble and the idea that such trouble may be surmounted by thinking clearly about and addressing its constituent parts. Among war surgeons, dauntlessness and pragmatism become points of pride. In 1915, it was not an approach particular to battle surgery. Physicians and surgeons in Montreal and Berlin and London and Paris dealt all day long with unexpected and unavoidable tragedy. Lethal meningococcal meningitis, injuries sustained in house fires, diphtheria, industrial accidents and tuberculosis were vastly more common then, and calmness in approaching them was just as important. The range and likelihood of fatal mischance might be the most important difference between our era and McCrae's. Today, people's children almost always survive. They didn't then. To a parent on either side of that difference, what could matter more? Death was closer to the average person then, and this fact says much about how a death-spewing war could be embraced so unflinchingly, by McCrae and by virtually all of his countrymen.

WAR SURGEONS MIGHT AFFECT a bring-it-on implacability, but the war itself cannot be put into that category of random trouble coming over the wall. It was not an accident, not an unavoidable threat. There was certainly never much of an attempt to avert it. The First World War was sought by the emperors, generals and prime ministers who had the power to avoid it, and by the deliriously delighted crowds in the street who urged them on. Anyone, like George Bernard Shaw or Bertrand Russell, who questioned the wisdom of the war was branded a traitor. Those who would die, such as McCrae, had mostly leapt up to fight. The boys and men who watched their intestines spill out of their abdomens had arrived thinking they would defend their countries from monsters, who in fact were other young men almost exactly like themselves. They had arrived thinking that spilling guts was just what they would do—to the other young men.

In retrospect, it is hard to grasp how shocking that murderous spasm was, coming after a mostly peaceful century for the British Empire and interrupting the Edwardian garden party of scientific and artistic ferment. Sometimes writers describe the war as having jolted the West out of a quiet slumber, but that isn't quite right. The blossoming of science and art already underway when the pistol was pointed at the carriage were revolutions themselves, exuberant and vital, even more so than the marching songs. The special theory of relativity had just emerged out of the Victorian steampunk tumult, and microbiology and cubist painting too. The world was being overturned anyway. And then war came and rolled it over a cliff.

In Canada, in peace, McCrae had been a physician consultant in infectious diseases, and he stood on the edge of that revolution in science. As a medical discipline, it is among the most intellectual. In the pre-antibiotic era, it was nearly purely academic. Once an infection was established, in McCrae's era, microbes chewed on flesh until there was no more to chew or the body had rallied itself. The nature of the involved microbe was the question infectious-disease specialists like McCrae addressed. In the years after the war, this discipline would produce the sulfonamide antibiotics, and then penicillin. Reflection is rewarded. But there were few useful interventions available to McCrae the physician.

Complexity, nuance and inference: enervating luxuries of peacetime.

—

WAR IS APHORISTICALLY HELL, and yet that hell is embraced. It is the central puzzle of "In Flanders Fields" and of a century of wars—First, Second, Cold, Gulf, Terror—that has not spared a single generation since McCrae re-enlisted. Contemporary readers avert their eyes from the third stanza of "In Flanders Fields," preferring to concentrate on the first two and drink the melancholy and grief within them. Some people even imagine that this is an anti-war poem—just as they imagine that professional soldiers fight reluctantly.

What McCrae wrote in the third stanza of "In Flanders Fields," entreating the living to "Take up our quarrel with the foe," is shocking. He adopts the voices of the dead, the men who have just lost the lives they were supposed to have lived— their children, the furniture they would have made, the houses they were to have built, the tender moments with their wives that were to have lingered as warming memories in their older years—and urges on more convulsive homicide. It is an act of astonishing and deluded presumption: Who would assume that, if the masses of war dead could speak—nearly twenty million in that conflagration—what they would urge on would be more of it? What sane person would suggest it?

If the delusion was isolated to this poem and its author, it would be easier to dismiss "In Flanders Fields" as the work of an especially skilled propagandist. And if it were that, it would be a less important and less achingly beautiful poem. The agony of "In Flanders Fields" begins with the comfortable initial stanzas and their melancholic whispers of the once-loved dead. It continues past that into the glazed-eyed endurance of their grief-stricken survivors: men such as McCrae, who paints an accidental and acutely revelatory self-portrait. In it, he looks away from the carnage all around him and repeats to himself,

"It has to be worth it. All this agony cannot possibly be for nothing." Even though, of course, it mostly was.

It isn't the way we think in peacetime. Unprofitable undertakings are abandoned, even and especially if much has been lost on them. A whole railway was left to sink into Newfoundland's muskeg, and still-new luxury ocean liners were scrapped when the airlines took to the skies. One hundred million MySpace pages just sit there.

But war is different from peace, surgery is different from medicine, and McCrae the surgeon was different from McCrae the physician. The soldier's and the surgeon's problems—bullet piercings and blasts—are seen and felt and smelled with an immediacy that shuts down consideration of larger issues. As Mike Tyson said, "Everyone has a plan until they get punched in the face." When violence is afoot, it and its consequences are all that matter. No one thinks clearly, which is just part of why war is so dangerous and how insidiously it perpetuates itself.

The eye—or rather the visual processing centre in the occipital cortex—is wired to be drawn to movement, to action. The neurology of this attention to motion has obvious Darwinian advantages. Trouble or prey in the shrubbery distinguishes itself by moving. Our hard-wired selves reward our conscious selves by making the survival duties pleasurable. The rush of adrenaline and the sympathetic enlivening surge young men feel on contemplating a run at the shrubbery make them feel the best they ever will.

We're hard-wired to be especially attentive to and excited by human conflict and threat. Primates are murderous. Once spears were invented, humans became, for other humans, the only mammalian menace that mattered; the company that protected us from the nighttime jackals became its own

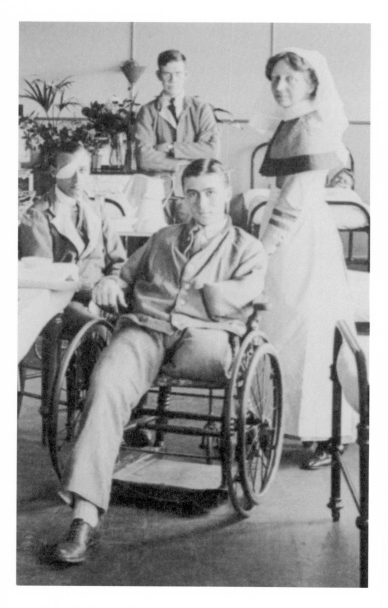

Surgery is battle, not poetry: Recovery ward, circa 1917, location unknown. Amputation was a fast solution, the decision to remove a limb made easier as the number of wounded climbed and the surgeon became more exhausted.

danger. Of course, we are aroused by the sound of angry human voices. When we respond to threat and feel that righteous rage surge through us, our unconscious selves reward us again for attending to the sentinel duties. Aspects of war are, in the moment, the most fun its participants ever know.

Our wiring suspends thoughtful reflection when violence erupts, and our limbic systems actively reward us just for imagining throwing the spear: the miracle is that we are not all constantly at war, in all places, all the time.

UNTIL ONLY ONE LONG lifetime ago, it was not possible to talk about unconscious drives and the havoc they wreak, because they had not themselves been contemplated. The other great intellectual revolution unfolding when the First World War came was psychoanalysis, though a man as resolute as McCrae may have disdained its insights. W.H.R. Rivers—like Freud, a neurologist—independently developed his psychoanalytic techniques to treat shell shock. He treated the war poets Siegfried Sassoon and Wilfred Owen successfully enough to send them back to the front. Owen was killed in action during the crossing of the Sambre–Oise Canal on November 4, 1918, seven days before the armistice. When he was in England being treated by Rivers, he wrote "Dulce et decorum est," and this is its last stanza:

If in some smothering dreams, you too could pace
Behind the wagon that we flung him in,
And watch the white eyes writhing in his face,
His hanging face, like a devil's sick of sin;
If you could hear, at every jolt, the blood
Come gargling from the froth-corrupted lungs

Obscene as cancer, bitter as the cud
Of vile, incurable sores on innocent tongues,—
My friend, you would not tell with such high zest
To children ardent for some desperate glory,
The old Lie: *Dulce et decorum est*
Pro patria mori.

Contemplate Owen and Sassoon, the infantry officers, sharing a beer with McCrae, the surgeon. What would the younger men, who did drink together, have made of McCrae and his poetry? It was McCrae, after all, who was published to great fame during the war; a work like "Dulce et decorum est" was not and could not have been published, even posthumously, until after the ceasefire. The less famous poets and junior officers would nevertheless have had the combat arms officer's swagger, which can be considerable. They might have thought themselves more interesting writers. Rank deference would have competed with young writers' disdain.

What would McCrae have made of them? If he knew about their shell shock, this would have given him pause. Any expressed opposition to the war would probably have concluded the conversation. But he could not have helped seeing the mastery in their writing. The Canadian McCrae may have envied them their access to the London literary circles. It could have been an interesting and electric conversation, but they would not have been likely to become close friends. They would have faced each other across a generational and artistic divide: modernists waving and pulling away from a Victorian romantic—McCrae back to his hospital, the infanteers to theirs, as patients. They were all injured.

Neurology was for Rivers and Freud like infectious diseases

were for McCrae. Neurology didn't yet offer many therapies. For the most part, it still doesn't; the preposterously complex vertebrate brain eludes detailed comprehension. But the profoundly empathic leap that psychotherapy represented, together with its therapeutic value—still superior to pills for everything except the most severe of depressions, bipolar disease and psychosis—makes it as momentous a development as penicillin.

Sometimes we ail as individuals, and sometimes we ail as whole populations, as in epidemics and famine. Sometimes whole societies fall victim to collective psychopathology. Depressions hung over the most damaged countries after both world wars, while the undamaged belligerents across the ocean had manic recoveries. The paranoia afoot in Stalin's Soviet Union defined him and his country for thirty years. The psychosis of Kim-era North Korea imprisons twenty-five million human beings in a delusional hell.

Belligerence in the face of conflict is as conscious or unconscious a response as other drives are. It can conceivably be suppressed. But the truth is that most of us can't or don't do it, and anyway, when the CNN theme music gets loud and Wolf Blitzer grows hyperbolic, we watch his animated maps with our transfixed and hard-wired eyes and feel the sympathetic surge that accompanies our blood lust. Those who escape or are able to defeat this response—Shaw, Russell, Owen, the Swiss—are too few really to matter. The rest of us give in. Opponents of wars, especially the disastrous ones of the last half century, are always so much more numerous in retrospect than they were at the moment of decision. When the troop starts to howl, joining in becomes irresistible, and then the troops are sent off amid not much voiced doubt at all. This happens over and over again. When the generals decide to make war, war gets made. One thing armies know how to do is to get us all howling.

In 1917, McCrae wrote his last poem, "The Anxious Dead." In it, he reassures his lost compatriots that "we will onward till we win or fall." It's the sort of language one might expect more from someone who has never seen what "falling" means. McCrae's language and sensibility are from the luxuriant peace of the nineteenth century. They celebrate derring-do and the dash of plucky old boys. The view was inseparable from McCrae's sensibility as a soldier. The horror immediately in front of him, on the other hand, was a matter for averted eyes.

Modernism was born in the trenches and arose in response to the inability of that Victorian sensibility to look in the face the horror it had wrought. Rudyard Kipling, one of the old lions, had spent two decades writing verse celebrating the martial spirit of the English Tommy—his influence on McCrae is apparent—but he could not recover from the death in action of his own son, John, who died in 1915 at Loos, the same year as the Second Battle of Ypres. This was his response to the loss: "If any question why we died / Tell them, because our fathers lied."

The old lion lived until 1936 but, gutted by his grief, never again wrote with the brio he had before the fighting began. Contemporary descriptions of McCrae describe a similar hollowing out in him after Ypres, and it seems clear he suffered too, though he was unable to express aloud doubt about the source of that suffering. Imagine what that felt like. The world had turned upside down for men such as these; their certitude had been so much of what they were.

The tension between McCrae the poet and McCrae the soldier was no less than that between his healer and soldier selves. The telling part is what he elided. Not for him any of Owen's "white eyes writhing in his face"—his concern was always that the dead "in content may turn them to their sleep." This idea of a contract between the glorious dead and the living, obliging the as-yet-unshattered to live up to the example shown them by their predecessors, recurs repeatedly in his war poetry. It is simultaneously evidence of a bloody obduracy and of the depth to which he was shaken by the loss he saw every day. The one thing that could make that loss even worse for him would be for it to be meaningless. He could not face that. And he didn't.

ERICH MARIA REMARQUE, in *All Quiet on the Western Front*, wrote, "A hospital alone shows what war is." McCrae knew what war is: A man is thrown to the ground and then he starts dying. He is brought to the hospital and a race ensues between the surgeon and the pumping severed arteries. Knowledge and intellect are helpful attributes for a trauma surgeon but are not more important than decisiveness and speed. As a surgeon, McCrae was able to—required to—dispense with reflection in favour of action. Surgery is violent and direct. Surgery is battle, not poetry.

In war surgery, the usefulness of reflection is eclipsed by that of nostrums and physical ability: Never close a battle wound primarily; they are always infected and will always abscess. Pus under pressure is lethal in any era and must be drained. A shot to the brain that crosses the midline is hopeless. Midline chest penetrations are fatal if not operated on immediately. Wide initial excision of devitalized tissue around wounds prevents wider and more mutilating surgery later.

These echo the principles of battle: Time on reconnaissance is never wasted. Don't bunch up. Don't skyline yourself. Know the state of your men's feet. Force your men to sleep before patrols. Never eat before they have. The worse the weather, the better the patrolling. Amateurs talk tactics, generals talk logistics.

It all takes on the reassuring cadence of liturgy. It might as well be sung in some dead language. Add in a Confucian worship of the dead, and the ancient cult, particular to the moment, is revived once again. The Huns destroyed Belgium and then they blew up the Bamiyan Buddhas. We are bringing civilization and order to the brutes. They are scumbags in need of killing. They raped all the nuns and won't let girls go to school; at heart we are feminists.

But make no mistake about our ferocity. Can't you hear how loudly we roar?

POPPIES HAVE BLOWN across Eurasia for millennia. They gave humans the one ancient drug we still widely use, the one that pierced soldiers need first and most. This need has propelled their spread; traders have brought poppy seeds along every camel track and into every port.

The beauty of poppies becomes most apparent in a breeze. The petals are larger than seem necessary and ripple like tendrils of torn cloth. A bright, living crimson is the most prevalent colour, but among the red are patches of white. In temperate latitudes, they will grow wild anywhere there is bright sun and reasonable drainage. They colonize hedgerows and the slopes of cleared hills. When they are cultivated in fields and subsequently viewed from drone or helicopter height, the crimson has a liquid intensity.

The intense colour of the flowers' petals was once a strategy to draw the attention of pollinators, but that hasn't mattered for thousands of years. Poppies prosper now because they have the ability to intoxicate humans, and the human thirst for this drug serves their purposes. In every port are men and women who have been ruined by them. But that doesn't matter either. If our appetite for intoxicants could be reasoned away, it would have been long ago.

Overleaf: Twins Pamela and Pauline Chamberlain
sell poppies, London, November 1953.

MARGARET ATWOOD
POPPIES: THREE VARIATIONS

In Flanders fields the poppies blow
Between the crosses, row on row.
   That mark our place; and in the sky
   The larks, still bravely singing, fly
Scarce heard amid the guns below.

JOHN MCCRAE

I.

I had an uncle once who served in Flanders. Flanders, or was it France? I'm old enough to have had the uncle but not old enough to remember. Wherever, those fields are green again, and plowed and harvested, though they keep throwing up rusty shells, broken skulls. The uncle wore a beret and marched in parades, though slowly. We always bought those felt poppies, which aren't even felt any more, but plastic: small red explosions pinned to your chest, like a blow to the heart. Between the other thoughts, that one crosses my mind. And the tiny lead soldiers in the shop windows, row on row of them, not lead any more, too poisonous, but every detail perfect, and from every part of the world: India, Africa, China,

Fall 2014: 888, 246 ceramic poppies, one for each British or colonial life lost in World War 1, were planted in the moat of the Tower of London. The installation's title, *Blood Swept Lands and Seas of Red*, was a quote from the will of an unknown soldier who died in Flanders.

America. That goes to show, about war—in retrospect it becomes glamour, or else a game we think we could have played better. From time to time the stores mark them down, you can get bargains. There are some for us, too, with our new leafy flag, not the red rusted-blood one the men fought under. That uncle had placemats with the old flag, and cups and saucers. The planes in the sky were tiny then, almost comical, like kites with wind-up motors; I've seen them in movies. The uncle said he never saw the larks. Too much smoke, or fog. Too much roaring, though on some mornings it was very still. Those were the most dangerous. You hoped you would act bravely when the moment came, you kept up your courage by singing. There was a kind of fly that bred in the corpses, there were thousands of them he said; and during the bombardments you could scarce hear yourself think. Though sometimes you heard things anyway: the man beside him whispered, "Look," and when he looked there was no more torso: just a red hole, a wet splotch in midair. That uncle's gone now too, the number of vets in the parade is smaller each year, they limp more. But in the windows the soldiers multiply, so clean and colorfully painted, with their little intricate guns, their shining boots, their faces, brown or pink or yellow, neither smiling nor frowning. It's strange to think how many soldiers like that have been owned over the years, loved over the years, lost over the years, in back yards or through gaps in porch floors. They're lying down there, under our feet in the garden and below the floorboards, armless or legless, faces worn half away, listening to everything we say, waiting to be dug up.

2.

Cup of coffee, the usual morning drug. He's off jogging, told
her she shouldn't be so sluggish, but she can't get organized,
it involves too many things: the right shoes, the right outfit,
and then worrying about how your bum looks, wobbling
along the street. She couldn't do it alone anyway, she might
get mugged. So instead she's sitting remembering how much
she can no longer remember, of who she used to be, who she
thought she would turn into when she grew up. We are the
dead: that's about the only line left from In Flanders Fields,
which she had to write out twenty times on the blackboard,
for talking. When she was ten and thin, and now see. He says
she should go vegetarian, like him, healthy as lettuce. She'd
rather eat poppies, get the opiates straight from the source.
Eat daffodils, the poisonous bulb like an onion. Or better,
slice it into his soup. He'll blow his nose on her once too
often, and then. Between the rock and the hard cheese, that's
where she sits, inert as a prisoner, making little crosses on the
wall, like knitting, counting the stitches row on row, that old
trick to mark off the days. Our place, he calls this dump. He
should speak for himself, she's just the mattress around here,
she's just the cleaning lady, and when he ever lifts a finger
there'll be sweet pie in the sky. She should burn the whole
thing down, just for larks; still, however bravely she may talk,
to herself, where would she go after that, what would she do?
She thinks of the bunch of young men they saw, downtown at
night, where they'd gone to dinner, his birthday. High on
something, singing out of tune, one guy's fly half open.
Freedom. Catch a woman doing that, panty alert, she'd be
jumped by every creep within a mile. Too late to make yourself
scarce, once they get the skirt up. She's heard of a case like

that, in a poolhall or somewhere. That's what keeps her in there, in this house, that's what keeps her tethered. It's not a midlife crisis, which is what he says. It's fear, pure and simple. Hard to rise above it. Rise above, like a balloon or the cream on milk, as if all it takes is hot air or fat. Or willpower. But the reason for that fear exists, it can't be wished away. What she'd need in real life is a few guns. That and the technique, how to use them. And the guts, of course. She pours herself another cup of coffee. That's her big fault: she might have the gun but she wouldn't pull the trigger. She'd never be able to hit a man below the belt.

3.

In school, when I first heard the word Flanders I thought it was what nightgowns were made of. And pajamas. But then I found it was a war, more important to us than others perhaps because our grandfathers were in it, maybe, or at least some sort of ancestor. The trenches, the fields of mud, the barbed wire, became our memories as well. But only for a time. Photographs fade, the rain eats away at statues, the neurons in our brains blink out one by one, and goodbye to vocabulary. We have other things to think about, we have lives to get on with. Today I planted five poppies in the front yard, orangey-pink, a new hybrid. They'll go well with the marguerites. Terrorists blow up airports, lovers slide blindly in between the sheets, in the soft green drizzle my cat crosses the street; in the spring regatta the young men row on, row on, as if nothing has happened since 1913, and the crowds wave and enjoy their tall drinks with cucumber and gin. What's wrong with that? We can scrape by, more or less, getting from year to year with hardly a mark on us, as long as we know our place, don't mouth off too much or cause uproars. A little sex, a little gardening, flush toilets and similar discreet pleasures; and in the sky the satellites go over, keeping a bright eye on us. The ospreys, the horned larks, the shrikes and the woodland warblers are having a thinner time of it, though still bravely trying to nest in the lacunae left by pesticides, the sharp blades of the reapers. If it's singing you want, there's lots of that, you can tune in any time; coming out of your airplane seatmate's earphones it sounds like a fly buzzing, it can drive you crazy. So can the news. Disaster sells beer, and this month hurricanes are the fashion, and famines: scarce this, scarce that, too little water, too much sun. With every mean you take huge bites of guilt. The excitement in the disembodied voices says: you heard it here first. Such a commotion in the mid-brain! Try meditation instead, be thankful for the annuals, for the smaller mercies. You listen, you listen to the moonlight, to the earthworms reveling in the lawn, you celebrate your own quick heartbeat. But below all that there's another sound, a groundswell, a drone, you can't get rid of it. It's the guns, which have never stopped, just moved around. It's the guns, still firing monotonously, bored with themselves but deadly, deadlier, deadliest, it's the guns, an undertone beneath each ordinary tender conversation. Say pass the sugar and you hear the guns. Say I love you. Put your ear against skin: below thought, below memory, below everything, the guns.

WADE DAVIS
OF WAR AND REMEMBRANCE

EVERYTHING YOU KNOW of your life, every sense you have of being modern, every existential doubt, each burst of confusion, every neurotic affirmation or affliction was born of the mud and blood of Flanders.

The Great War was the fulcrum of modernity. Jazz, Joyce, Dali, Cocteau, Hitler, Mao and Stalin were all offspring of the carnage. Darwin, Freud and Einstein were men of the nineteenth century, but their deeply unorthodox ideas—that species are mutable, that you do not control the sanctity of your own thoughts, that an apple does not fall from the tree as simply as Newton described—came to fruition and achieved general acceptance in the wake of the conflict, as if sown in soil fertilized by the dead.

For a century, Europe had been at peace even as industry and technology generated wealth and military power beyond anything that had ever been known. European nations consumed the world until the boundaries of colonial ambitions met and slowly tightened around the neck of civilization. Then a single bullet fired into the breast of a prince in Sarajevo in the summer of 1914 shattered a universe, a realm of certainty, optimism, hope and faith, and in doing so sparked the greatest cataclysm in the history of humanity.

Beaumont-Hamel, France, 1916. On the first day of the Battle of the Somme, 810 Newfoundlanders went over the top. Thirty-five survived.

For a desperate month, people of all nations held their breath as those in power, no more than a hundred men, decided their fate. Hope for peace was bitterly betrayed. Born of another century, incapable of understanding a world that in a generation had been transformed by science, Europe's leaders were outflanked by history. With their peacock vanities and wrathful pride, their misplaced fidelities and pious certainties, cursed by a fatal and antiquated sense of honour, they stumbled toward the final hour before plunging their civilization into an abyss from which it would never emerge. The Second World War was but the child of the First. Winston Churchill called it another Thirty Years' War. Never was there a war less necessary to fight than the first, he wrote, or more essential to win than the second. But it was all, he recognized, a single spasm of destruction.

At the outbreak of the conflict, in August of 1914, a man had to stand five feet eight inches to enter the British Army. Within two months, boys of five feet three were eagerly recruited. In eight weeks, the British Expeditionary Force, four divisions that represented the entire home army of the British Empire, had been virtually annihilated. In the first month of the war, the French lost seventy thousand men, forty thousand alone over two terrible days in August. Every month, the British Army required ten thousand junior officers alone to replace the litany of dead. Public schools graduated their senior classes not to Oxford or Cambridge but directly to the trenches. The chance of any British boy aged thirteen to twenty-four surviving the war in 1914 was one in three.

For the men in the trenches, the world became a place of mud and sky, with only the zenith sun to remind the living that they had not already been buried and left for dead. The regular army of the British Empire required 2,500 shovels a year. In the mud of Flanders, ten million would be required. Twenty-five thousand British coal miners spent the war underground, ferreting beneath the German lines to lay charges that detonated with such explosive force as to be heard on Hampstead Heath in London.

The sepia images that inform memories of the war, the tens of thousands of photographs taken in what was the first industrial conflict to be thoroughly documented on film, remain haunting and powerfully evocative. But the visual medium fails to capture two of the most dominant features of life at the front: the sound and the smell, the soul-crushing noise of prolonged bombardments and the constant stench in the trenches, an unholy combination of sweat, fear, blood, cordite, excrement, vomit and putrescence. Staged images of men advancing, rifles and bayonets at the ready, belie the horror of helplessness that men actually experienced in an attack. Bayonets accounted for but a third of 1 per cent of casualties. Rifle fire and machine guns brought down 35 per cent of the dead and wounded. Most who died did so clinging in terror to the mud wall of a trench as a rain of steel and fire fell from the sky.

The concentration of suffering was unprecedented, in part because the zone of military operations was so small. For much of the war, the British front was a mere 85 miles in length, and at no time did it exceed 125 miles. Indeed, the entire British sector, in which millions of men lived, trained and died, extended only 50 by 60 miles, roughly the size of the English county of Lincolnshire. To supply and defend roughly a hundred miles of war front, the British would dig more than six thousand miles of trenches and lay down six thousand miles of railroad. The Ypres Salient in Belgium—a section of the battlefield

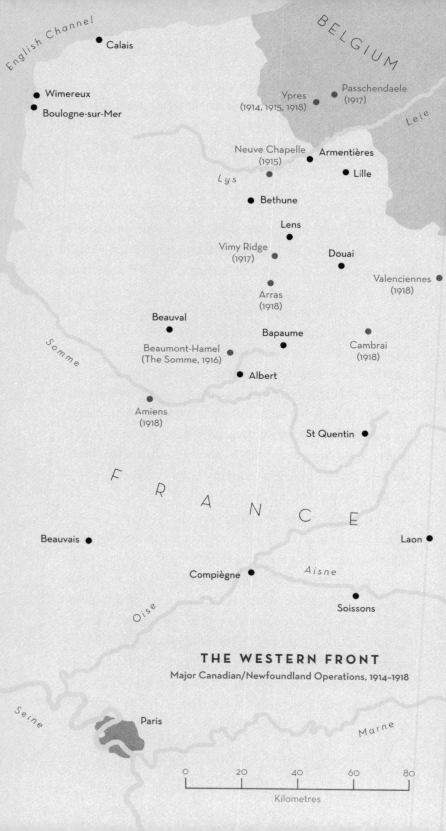

English Channel

BELGIUM

Calais

Wimereux

Boulogne-sur-Mer

Ypres
(1914, 1915, 1918)

Passchendaele
(1917)

Leie

Neuve Chapelle
(1915)

Armentières

Lille

Lys

Bethune

Lens

Vimy Ridge
(1917)

Douai

Valenciennes
(1918)

Arras
(1918)

Beauval

Bapaume

Somme

Beaumont-Hamel
(The Somme, 1916)

Cambrai
(1918)

Albert

Amiens
(1918)

St Quentin

F R A N C E

Beauvais

Laon

Compiègne

Aisne

Oise

Soissons

THE WESTERN FRONT

Major Canadian/Newfoundland Operations, 1914–1918

Seine

Paris

Marne

0   20   40   60   80

Kilometres

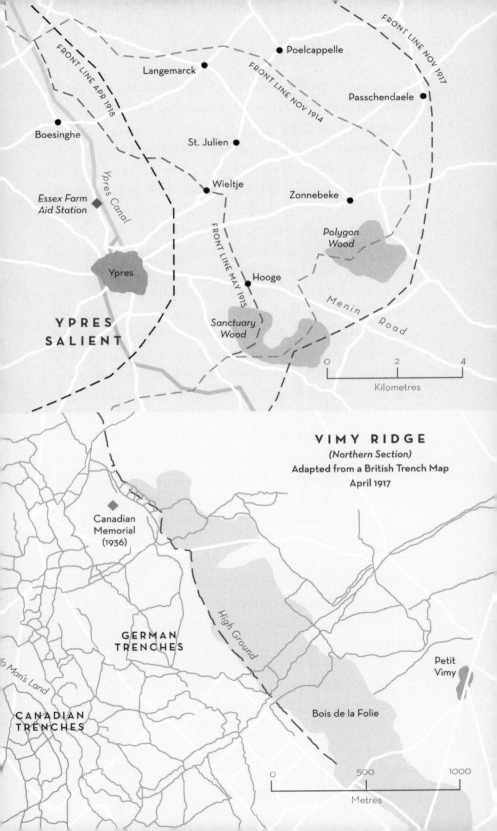

FRONT LINE NOV 1917

FRONT LINE APR 1918

Poelcappelle

Langemarck

FRONT LINE NOV 1914

Passchendaele

Boesinghe

St. Julien

Ypres Canal

Essex Farm
Aid Station

Wieltje

Zonnebeke

Polygon
Wood

FRONT LINE MAY 1915

Ypres

**YPRES
SALIENT**

Hooge

Sanctuary
Wood

Menin

Road

0   2   4
Kilometres

VIMY RIDGE
(Northern Section)
Adapted from a British Trench Map
April 1917

Canadian
Memorial
(1936)

High Ground

Petit
Vimy

**GERMAN
TRENCHES**

Man's Land

Bois de la Folie

**CANADIAN
TRENCHES**

0   500   1000
Metres

surrounded on three sides by German forces—measured four miles by twelve; in that cauldron of death, 1.7 million boys and men would fall.

Among them would be many of the Canadian troops who sailed for England in the first week of October 1914. A British declaration of war had implied the participation of the dominions, and Canada, Australia, New Zealand and South Africa rallied to the colours. The lads of Newfoundland, then a separate colony, sailed from St. John's on October 4 on HMS *Florizel*, heading through the Narrows and south to a rendez-vous in the darkness with a flotilla of thirty-one ships. They were escorted by the twenty-six-thousand-ton battle cruiser *Princess Royal*, which was transporting to England the 1st Canadian Division, along with nearly seven thousand horses. The Atlantic crossing took eleven days. Following disembarkation at Plymouth, the force was transported to a training camp at Salisbury Plain. There they remained through a long fall and wet winter, soaked by two feet of rain in four months, twice the normal precipitation, as they drilled and marched and practised all the skills deemed essential in the military training manuals, few of which would serve any purpose in France.

The Newfoundland Regiment was dispatched to Gallipoli and the Canadians went to France, arriving in time to plug the British line at the Second Battle of Ypres. They were there on April 22, 1915, when the Germans attacked using poison gas for the first time in the history of warfare. Geoffrey Winthrop Young, a volunteer in the base hospital, recalled the day.

> The bombardment seemed heavier and more menacing. . . .
> I walked uneasily through our wards and offices. A wounded
> soldier, in the half coma we knew later as shell shock, was

being tended and was muttering continuously "White faces
. . . the moonlight . . . white faces." . . . I went out. I could see
figures running back, the yellow pall of cloud was higher,
and again dots of figures in khaki were hurrying forward
across the fields out to the northeast of us. . . . The wounded
began to pour in . . . the first poison gas sufferers. This
horror was too monstrous to believe at first. . . . But when it
came, far as we had travelled from our civilized world of a
few months back, the savagery of it, of the sight of men
choking to death with yellow froth, lying on the floor and
out on the fields, made me rage with an anger which no later
cruelty of man, not even the degradation of our kind by the
hideous concentration camps in later Germany, ever quite
rekindled; for then we still thought all men were human.

If the Germans had stooped to a new low, the reputation of
the Canadians soared to new heights, for it was only their heroic
defence that stopped the assault at Ypres and held the British
line, even as Allied forces on all sides panicked and fled the
field. This was the beginning of what can only be seen as the
transformation of a nation due to the martial skills of its
soldiers. As the Canadian Expeditionary Force grew into a corps
of four divisions, with over 400,000 men serving overseas, it
proved to be not just a formidable fighting force but arguably
the most innovative and imaginative command in the Allied
armies. The battle roll reads as a complete record of the Western
Front. In 1915, Canadians fought at Neuve Chapelle in March,
Ypres in April, endured the collapse at Aubers Ridge in May and
in September the disaster at Loos, a battle known to the
Germans as *Der Leichenfeld von Loos*, the Corpse Field of Loos.

Then came the Somme in the summer of 1916. In 140 days,

the British advanced the line just six miles, leaving the Allies four miles short of Bapaume, which the General Staff had anticipated capturing on the opening day of the campaign. The British had in place 1,537 batteries, each capable of firing a thousand rounds a day.

As a prelude to the attack, for seven days the British unleashed a bombardment that grew to a sustained hurricane of piercing screams that hovered day and night over the entire length of the front. An NCO of the 22nd Manchester Rifles who survived the battle, later recalled,

> The sound was different, not only in magnitude but in quality, from anything known to me. . . . It hung over us. It seemed as though the air were full of vast and agonized passion, bursting now with groans and sighs, now into shrill screaming and pitiful whimpering, shuddering beneath terrible blows, torn by unearthly whips, vibrating with the solemn pulses of enormous wings. And the supernatural tumult did not pass in this direction or in that. It did not begin, intensify, decline and end. It was poised in the air, a stationary panorama of sound, a condition of the atmosphere, not the creation of man.

At the front, the Allied troops stumbled as the ground shook through their boots. A Canadian private wrote that "one's whole body seemed to be in a mad macabre dance. . . . I felt that if I lifted a finger I should touch a solid ceiling of sound, it now had the attribute of solidity." Thirty million shells were fired, 600,000 Germans were killed or wounded, and after four months the battlefield, a few score square miles, was covered in layers upon layers of corpses, three and four deep, bodies bloated, bones sticking up randomly from the ground, faces black with bluebottle flies.

To lie helpless in a trench in the midst of such an assault was, as one soldier recalled, like being tied to a post and attacked by an enemy wielding a sledgehammer. The hammer swings back for the blow, whirls forward, till, "just missing your skull, it sends the splinters flying from the post once more. This is exactly what it feels like to be exposed to heavy shelling." The blood rises to the head, fever burns the body, nerves, stretched to their limit, break. Men lose control, whimper and moan, and their eyes sink deep into sockets that will never again know the light.

And then there was the constant smell of decaying flesh, what remained of men caught on the wire, drowned in mud, choked by the oily slime of gas, reduced to a spray of red mist, quartered limbs hanging from shattered branches of burnt trees, bodies swollen and blackened skulls gnawed by rats, corpses stuck in the sides of trenches that aged with each day into the colours of the dead. Assigned to dig a communication trench to Devil's Wood in the wake of an afternoon attack that had left four thousand dead, the commander of a British detachment went mad, as he found himself digging not through the chalk soils of Picardy but through bodily remains of those who had fallen in earlier attacks, cadavers stacked six feet deep, all of which fell apart to the touch.

At the Somme, the Canadians fought for four months, but the boys of Newfoundland perished in an hour. The regiment had returned from Gallipoli on the eve of the battle. Attached to the British 29th Division, charged with the task of assaulting an impregnable fortress at Beaumont-Hamel, the Newfoundland Regiment was ordered over the top at 9:15 a.m. on July 1, the opening day of the battle. Their right flank hung in the air, because the 1st Battalion of the Essex Regiment, the next unit in line, had been delayed reaching the starting point by the sheer volume of dead. The lads barely got out of their own trench, and when they did, they floundered and died at their own parapet, their ranks swept by German machine gun fire. Those few who advanced slowed and faltered, burdened by their loads, leaning and bowing into the storm as if to limit exposure to the lead. The British artillery barrage, timed to the second, had long since moved ahead and away from the immediate battlefield. Men dropped dead at every yard and still the regiment pressed on. A few miraculously reached the German line, only to be shot down in the mud or skewered on the wire, which was not cut. Indeed, the last thought of many of these brave men, breathless with exhaustion, blood whipped and deranged with fear, was the horrid realization that the German line was utterly unscathed. Nothing had been damaged at all. The preliminary bombardment had missed. In fury, they spun into the wire, tossing grenades, their screams baffled by the throaty gurgle men sound when hit in the brain.

Altogether, 810 men of the Newfoundland Regiment went over the top that morning. Just thirty-five emerged from the battle physically unscathed. Every officer was lost, including three who should not have been in the attack at all. Only the commander and his adjutant survived to hear the praise of the General Staff. "It was a magnificent display of trained and disciplined valour," a senior staff officer told the Newfoundland prime minister, "and its assault only failed of success because dead men can advance no further."

In the wake of the Somme, the Canadian forces came together under a single command rather than acting as reinforcements for the Allied lines, and for the rest of the war the corps fought under the leadership of a Canadian, Sir Arthur Currie. If the British were led by men whose minds ran on rails and who sacrificed their soldiers as if on a mission to reduce the national population, General Currie brought insight and invention to the battlefield, qualities that resulted in one of the great Allied victories of the war, at Arras, in the spring of 1917.

The low fields of Flanders were flat and water soaked, with few features rising more than two hundred feet above sea level. The slightest hill took on strategic importance. Looming over the British line was one dominant escarpment, five miles in length and rising nearly five hundred feet above the battlefield. The Germans had seized the heights of Vimy Ridge in 1914 and repulsed every subsequent British and French attack. Thousands had perished, and with each passing month the position became more formidable as the Germans reinforced the command and enhanced defensive fortifications.

On Easter Monday, April 9, the Canadian Corps, 170,000 strong and fighting together as a single force for the first time, went over the top. Without benefit of a preliminary bombardment, with new tactics that favoured surprise and initiative, they overwhelmed the German defences and within a day had taken most of the heights. Within three days, Vimy Ridge was theirs. It was the singular triumph of the Battle of Arras. Casualties included 3,598 killed and 7,004 wounded, terrible losses but modest by the standards of the war, especially given the scale and significance of the victory.

The unprecedented conquest at Vimy Ridge secured the reputation of the Canadian Corps, but it also meant that for the rest of the war the force would serve as the shock troops for the Allied cause. Not four months later, the corps was

The remains of a German soldier at Beaumont-Hamel, the Somme, 1916. There would have been thousands of bodies scattered across the battlefield, each decomposing at various rates, depending on which parts of the corpse were exposed to the elements and scavenging wildlife. Ernest Brooks, a British war photographer who took this picture, refuted claims that the positioning of these remains was somehow unnatural, and affirmed that official photographers were under strict orders never to fake any such scenes.

Reporting on the outcome of the first day of the Somme, a senior officer told the Newfoundland Prime Minister that ". . . its assault only failed of success because dead men can advance no further."

transferred to Ypres to take part in Passchendaele, a battle that would be remembered by the historian A.J.P. Taylor as "the blindest slaughter of a blind war."

The goal was yet another fantasy of the British high command, a plan to break out of the Ypres Salient and capture Antwerp and the channel ports of Belgium. For the British and Canadian soldiers, it was the worst battle of the war. The ground was flat, sodden, shattered by shellfire. On the first night of the assault, the last day in July, the rains began, and, except for a brief respite in September, they did not cease until November. Three thousand Allied guns fired more than four million explosive shells, nearly five tons of high explosive for every yard of German trench. The result was a muddy quagmire, a sea of black waste and shell holes, carcasses of horses and men, clouds of yellow and brown mist, an unbearable stench of rot and gangrene and the sweet scent of violets, which was the smell of gas and thus also the odour of death. To slip, wounded, off a duckboard was to drown in the fathomless morass. Gunners worked thigh-deep in water. To advance over open ground, soldiers used the bodies of the dead as stepping stones. On the day after the final assault, a senior British staff officer, Lieutenant-General Sir Launcelot Kiggell, made his first ever visit to the front. Reaching as far as his car could advance, appalled by the conditions, he began to weep. "Good God," he said, "did we really send men to fight in that?" The man beside him, who had been in action, replied flatly, "It's much worse farther up."

After three months, during which time the British suffered some 400,000 casualties, the village of Passchendaele, the objective of the first morning, had yet to fall. Once again, as at the Somme, it was noted in official documents that the British

Army lacked the clerk power to tabulate the dead. The German high command compared Passchendaele to Verdun, a battle where more than a million French and German soldiers had been killed or severely wounded. "The horror of Verdun," wrote German general Erich Ludendorff, "was surpassed. It was no longer life at all. It was mere unspeakable suffering. And through this world of mud the attackers dragged themselves, slowly but steadily, and in dense masses. Caught in the advance zone of our hail of fire they often collapsed, and the lonely man in the shell hole breathed again."

The Germans simply fell back to a second and third line of defence. British generals begged their commander, General Haig, to call off the attack, but he refused. The village of Passchendaele fell to the Canadians on November 6. When the onset of winter finally drowned out the guns, Haig asked Sidney Clive, his senior liaison to French headquarters, "Have we really lost half a million men?" He had, for an advance of five miles. The corpses of more than ninety thousand British and Canadian dead at Passchendaele were recovered too severely mutilated to be identified. Forty-two thousand disappeared without a trace.

By the spring of 1918, the greatest security challenge for the Allied command was concealing the location of the Canadian Corps, whose presence at any sector of the front implied to the Germans an imminent assault. During the German Spring Offensive of 1918, the Canadians reinforced the French and British up and down the line. Then, in August, the Canadian Corps spearheaded the Allied counteroffensive at Amiens, the battle that turned the tide on the Western Front. The Canadians overwhelmed the enemy trenches, inflicting a defeat that caused Ludendorff to call August 8 "the black day of the

German army." It was the beginning of what became known as Canada's Hundred Days, a nonstop engagement as the Allied forces, with the Canadian Corps in the vanguard, pushed the Germans east until their final surrender. The carnage continued until the end. The British and Canadian forces lost 300,000 men in just the final three months of the war. The guns fired literally until the eleventh hour. One of the last Allied soldiers to die was a Canadian private, George Lawrence Price, killed two minutes before the armistice went into effect. When word of the armistice spread up and down the line on November 11, it was greeted with relief and jubilation leavened by numb exhaustion, like the slow fading of a long and violent hallucination. The Allies had been preparing for another two years of war; many simply thought it would go on forever.

THE OLD MEN who had talked their nations into a war they could not escape had no idea of what they had wrought. For the moment, it seemed a tremendous victory. Germany and its allies lay prostrate. Russia was convulsed in upheaval and revolution, and France bled white and reeling from losses from which it might never recover as a nation. The British emerged from the conflict with the most powerful army in the world, its navy supreme, its empire enhanced by a surge of colonial acquisitions that would not end until 1935, when it would finally reach its greatest geographical extent. That the war had destroyed the prosperity of a century of progress was not immediately evident to the average civilian still marching to the rhythms of tradition. That it had birthed the nihilism and alienation of a new century was a thought impossible to anticipate.

The truth lay in the numbers. Nearly a million dead in Britain and the dominions alone, some 2.5 million wounded, 40,000 amputees, 60,000 without sight, 2.4 million on disability a decade after the end, including 65,000 men who never recovered from the "twilight memory of hell" that was shell shock. In France, fully 75 per cent of all men and boys between the ages of eighteen and thirty were either killed or wounded in the war. Quite literally, an entire generation was sacrificed to the carnage.

The victory had in fact bankrupted Britain. Before the war, the total cost of running the British Empire was roughly £500,000 a day. The war would cost £5 million a day. Taxes and death duties alone provoked such economic agonies that between 1918 and 1921 a quarter of all English land would change hands. Nothing like it had occurred in Britain since the Norman Conquest.

For a decade, the social impact of the war spread as a slow wave throughout the far reaches of the Empire. Cremation, virtually unknown in Britain, Canada and Australia before the war, became the preferred form of disposing of the dead for tens of thousands who had endured the sight and scent of death in the shell holes of no man's land. Daily exposure to that horror made cremation seem a clean, pure and highly desirable alternative to burial.

Plastic surgery was also born of the war and the need to repair the shell-scarred faces of young boys who would live their lives behind wooden masks, attending special holiday camps where they might feel the wind on their gargoyle features without shame or humiliation.

If a generation of men had been lost, a generation of women had been left with few prospects for marriage and families. Single women, often travelling with a female companion, became a familiar sight on British trains and certainly a cliché of travel literature and popular culture.

Many people spoke of the war through the metaphor of dance. "By the end of 1916," Diana Manners famously remarked, "every boy I had ever danced with was dead." Vera Brittain, who lost her brother, fiancé and two best friends, said simply that by the end of the war there was no one left to dance with. The poet Stephen Spender remarked that the British middle class continued to dance, unaware that the dance floor had fallen out from beneath them.

IN EARLY 1919, the British government formed a Peace Committee to determine how properly to commemorate the victory. Their initial meeting, chaired by the foreign secretary, Lord Curzon, proposed a four-day celebration to be held in August 1919. Deemed a waste of money by veterans and with thousands of soldiers still awaiting demobilization, the event was scaled back to a single parade, scheduled for July 19. Tens of thousands of citizens descended on London to watch fifteen thousand servicemen parade past a temporary wood and plaster monument erected in Whitehall, a cenotaph dedicated to "The Glorious Dead." Had the actual dead walked abreast down Whitehall, the parade would have lasted more than four days. Had each man who died in the war been granted a single page upon which to inscribe his life, it would have yielded a library of some twenty thousand volumes, each six hundred pages long.

The men who had fought in the trenches encountered peace on very different terms. For many, as Paul Fussell wrote in The Great War and Modern Memory, travel became a source of irrational happiness, a moving celebration of the sheer joy of being alive. For these men, England offered only a memory of lost youth, betrayal and lies, the residue of "four years of repression, casualty lists and mass murder sanctioned by Bishops." The poet and composer Ivor Gurney had been gassed and wounded, and he died in 1937 still believing that the battle raged and he was part of it. Before his descent into madness, he had a moment of clarity. Returning from the front, and before he was institutionalized, he set out from Gloucester on foot to find a ship, any ship, that might take him away. H.M. Tomlinson, who nearly froze to death at Ypres, and whose memory was haunted by shellfire splintering the marble earth of winter, escaped as soon as he could to bask in the Caribbean sun and write exquisite elegies of the tropics. Maurice Wilson, who earned the Military Cross at Passchendaele and later had his arm and chest ripped open by machine gun fire, a wound that never healed, wandered the South Pacific for a decade before conceiving a wild scheme to climb Mount Everest by fasting and mystic levitation. He bought a Gipsy Moth, learned to fly, and managed to reach Darjeeling, where he sold his biplane and, accompanied by two Sherpa guides, began the walk that would lead to his solitary death on the ice of the mountain.

Those who did go home, veterans who had lost years of their lives and endured unspeakable hardships, returned to a nation that wanted to forget everything about the war. They, too, wanted to forget. The poet Robert Graves and his friend T.E. Lawrence (who would eventually become known around the world as Lawrence of Arabia) famously made a pact never to speak of it. What they wanted was quiet. But, for Graves at least, as for many, it was impossible to escape the memories. There was always the night, waking in a pool of sweat, visions of bayonets and blood. Graves had enlisted at nineteen in the Royal Welch Fusiliers at the outbreak of the war. On July 20, 1916, in a reserve trench awaiting an attack on High Wood at the Somme, his battalion was caught by German artillery fire that left a third of the men dead and Graves seriously wounded. A metal splinter split his finger to the bone. Another metal shard went through his thigh, near the groin. Yet a third piece of shrapnel pierced his chest, slicing a hole through his body, destroying his right lung. Unconscious, he was carried to a dressing station and left among the dead. Notice of his passing reached his mother four days later, on what would have been his twenty-first birthday. His name appeared in the "honour roll" of the *Times*. But Graves in fact had survived the first night, and when the burial detail came by on the morning of July 21, he was found to be breathing. In agony, he was carried to a casualty clearing station, where, because of the sheer numbers of wounded, he lay on a stretcher in the summer heat for five days before finally being evacuated to a hospital at Rouen and then by ship and train to London. Two days later, he arrived at Victoria station—immortalized by photographer Francis James Mortimer as the "Gate of Goodbye"—where the living and the dying crossed paths and crowds gathered throughout the war to receive the wounded home from the front.

Such an experience left Graves mentally unprepared for peace. He remained, as he recalled in *Goodbye to All That*, nervously organized for war. Shells burst above his bed as he slept. Strangers in the street assumed the faces of friends lost at the front. He could not use a telephone. Train travel made him ill. To encounter more than two people in a day cost him his sleep. He could not walk in a field without reading the lay of the land as if on a raid. The sound of thunder made him shake. A sharp report of any kind, the backfiring of a car, the slamming of a door, flung him face first to the ground. The smell of cut lumber recalled the blasted pines and the corpses suspended from broken snags. His marriage dissolved and he left England for

Majorca, never to return to live in his native land.

On the war, Robert Graves remained mute, as did so many of his generation, simply because language itself had failed them. Words did not exist to describe what they had endured. After the war, as John Masefield wrote, one needed a new term for mud, a new word for death. The artist Paul Nash wrote that sunsets and sunrises had become "mockeries to man," blasphemous moments, preludes to death. Only the wordless, said Virginia Woolf, "are the happy." And only those who had fought understood. "The man who really endured the War at its worst," wrote Siegfried Sassoon, "was everlastingly differentiated from everyone but his fellow soldiers."

A graduate of Marlborough College and the University of Cambridge, a published poet and son of the landed gentry, Sassoon lived until 1967, but he would never write of anything that occurred after 1920. His six volumes of autobiography are the stories of a life that ended with the war. He expressed his anguish in verse, for his was a generation that still celebrated poetry as a real and meaningful literary form. The British Empire's elation at the outbreak of the conflict and its final descent to despair is readily tracked in the three most famous poems of the war: "The Soldier," by Rupert Brooke, John McCrae's "In Flanders Fields" and Wilfred Owen's master-piece, "Dulce et decorum Est."

Described by W.B. Yeats as a golden-haired Apollo, the most handsome man in England, Rupert Brooke, like many of his peers, rallied to the flag in the fall of 1914. "We have," he told a friend, "come into our heritage." He joined the navy and later witnessed the siege of Antwerp. Three months into the conflict, the glory was gone. "It's a bloody thing," he wrote on November 5. "Half the youth of Europe blown through pain to nothingness, in the incessant mechanical slaughter of these modern battles. I can only marvel at human endurance." Upon his return to England, Brooke wrote "The Soldier."

If I should die, think only this of me:
That there's some corner of a foreign field
That is forever England. There shall be
In that rich earth a richer earth concealed;
A dust whom England bore, shaped, made aware,
Gave, once, her flowers to love, her ways to roam;
A body of England's, breathing English air,
Washed by the rivers, blest by suns of home.

The poem, along with four other of Brooke's sonnets, was published in 1914 and Other Poems, a slim volume that in five years would go through twenty-eight printings. Brooke did not live to see its success. En route to Gallipoli from Egypt, his ship stopped off at the island of Skyros on Saturday, April 17, 1915, where, feverish, he wandered for several hours through olive groves scented with thyme and sage. By Thursday morning, April 22, he was comatose, his temperature rising by late afternoon to 106. The following day, he was dead of sepsis, brought on by an infected mosquito bite. He was buried in a "corner of a foreign field" on Skyros.

John McCrae was an older man, forty-three at the beginning of the war, a Canadian surgeon who served near Ypres in the terrible spring of 1915. Unlike Brooke, McCrae saw the worst of the fighting. The stress on such medical officers was intense and unrelenting. They were encouraged by social convention, decency and military orders to do all that was possible to maintain good cheer. At the same time, as surgeons they had to deal with an endless flow of carnage, working throughout the night as the guns roared and the flares and star shells lit up the sky, silhouetting ghostly figures in khaki wrapped in bloody blankets, labels dangling from limp bodies carried into tents where the flicker of acetylene lamps cast barely enough light for the doctors to distinguish the nature of the wounds.

In May, following the death of young Canadian officer and friend Alexis Helmer, McCrae wrote the fifteen lines of the poem that, more than any other, would distill the anguish of 1915, a time when there still remained hope that the conflict ultimately would have some redemptive meaning. He chose as a symbol of remembrance a delicate flower, unaware of the cruel irony that poppies flourished in the fields of Flanders only because constant shelling and rivers of blood had transformed the chemistry of the soil. "In Flanders Fields" survived the war, but McCrae did not. He died of pneumonia and meningitis at Wimereux, France, on January 28, 1918.

Brooke's and McCrae's poetry, with its invocations of duty and honour, sacrifice and redemption, served the needs of a British government increasingly concerned about unrest and discontent on the home front. As early as the end of August 1914, the chancellor of the exchequer, David Lloyd George, and the foreign secretary, Edward Grey, had established the secret War Propaganda Bureau, the goal of which was to promote British war aims, both at home and abroad. In 1917, the Propaganda Bureau was taken over by the Department of Information. By then, as Lloyd George, who had become prime minister, acknowledged, the "terrible losses without appreciable results had spread a general sense of disillusionment and war weariness throughout the nation." In a remark to C.P. Scott of the *Manchester Guardian* in December 1917, the prime minister added, "If the people really knew, the war would be stopped tomorrow." The task of the Department of Information was to ensure that they did not know. In this, the closest allies of the government were the newspapers. Anything might be written as long as it vilified the enemy and propped up morale. "So far as Britain is concerned," recalled John Buchan, head of the department, "the war could not have been fought for one month without its newspapers." The truth itself became a casualty. "While some patriots went to the battle front and died for their country," wrote A.R. Buchanan, "others stayed home and lied for it."

It was precisely this duplicity that led Siegfried Sassoon to come out against the war in the summer of 1917. Wounded by a sniper's bullet through the chest, and later shot accidentally in the head by one of his own men, Sassoon had received the Military Cross and the Distinguished Service Order (DSO), medals he would one day toss away into the Mersey. He had been deemed a hero, which made it especially awkward when his powerful manifesto was published in the *Times*.

I am making this statement as an act of willful defiance of military authority because I believe the war is being deliberately prolonged by those who have the power to end it. I am a soldier, convinced that I am acting on behalf of soldiers. I believe that this war, upon which I entered as a war of defence and liberation, has now become a war of aggression and conquest. . . . On behalf of those who are suffering now, I make this protest against the deception that is being practiced on them; also I believe that I may help destroy the callous complacency with which the majority of those at home regard the continuance of agonies which they do not share, and which they have not sufficient imagination to realise.

For a serving officer to publish such a tract was tantamount to treason. To avoid the embarrassment of a military court martial, the government agreed to a compromise suggested by Robert Graves. Sassoon would be declared mentally unfit, and dispatched to Craiglockhart, a military hospital in Edinburgh that specialized in the treatment of officers suffering from neurasthenia, or shell shock. It was there that he met Wilfred Owen. Owen had joined the 2nd Manchesters in December 1916 and within a week was at the front, "marooned on a frozen desert," lying beside the stiff bodies of friends dead from the cold. For twelve days, he did not sleep, wash or remove his boots. Under constant gas and artillery attack, with shells bursting within yards of his position, burying comrades alive, Owen shattered. He endured another three months until, shaking and tremulous, his memory vacant, he was evacuated from the front.

At Craiglockhart, Owen showed some of his unpublished poetry to Sassoon, who encouraged him to write about the war as the soldier actually experienced it. Inspired, Owen composed six poems in a single week. Among them was "Dulce et decorum est," considered by many to be the greatest anti-war poem ever written. The title comes from Horace, a line that had been inscribed in public school minds for generations. "It is sweet and proper to die for one's country."

Bent double, like old beggars under sacks,
Knock-kneed, coughing like hags, we cursed through sludge,
Till on the haunting flares we turned our backs
And towards our distant rest began to trudge.
Men marched asleep. Many had lost their boots
But limped on, blood-shod. All went lame; all blind;

Drunk with fatigue; deaf even to the hoots
Of tired, outstripped Five-Nines that dropped behind.

Gas! GAS! Quick, boys!—An ecstasy of fumbling,
Fitting the clumsy helmets just in time;
But someone still was yelling out and stumbling,
And flound'ring like a man in fire or lime . . .
Dim, through the misty panes and thick green light,
As under a green sea, I saw him drowning.

In all my dreams, before my helpless sight,
He plunges at me, guttering, choking, drowning.

If in some smothering dreams you too could pace
Behind the wagon that we flung him in,
And watch the white eyes writhing in his face,
His hanging face, like a devil's sick of sin;
If you could hear, at every jolt, the blood
Come gargling from the froth-corrupted lungs,
Obscene as cancer, bitter as the cud
Of vile, incurable sores on innocent tongues,
My friend, you would not tell with such high zest
To children ardent for some desperate glory,
The old Lie: *Dulce et decorum est*
Pro patria mori.

Wilfred Owen returned to the trenches and later would win
the Military Cross by singlehandedly seizing a German machine
gun and using it to kill more of the enemy than he wished to
remember. He would die seven days before the end of the war,
leading his men in an attack across the Sambre–Oise Canal.

Word of his death would reach his parents at Shrewsbury on November 11, 1918, as the church bells in their village tolled the news of victory and the armistice.

WITH THE PEACE, two million parents in Britain and the dominions woke to the realization that their sons were dead, even as the first of some three million veterans returned to a land socially and politically dominated by those who had not served. "I simply could not speak to such people," recalled Captain Herbert Read, who lost a brother in the last month of the war and was himself awarded the Military Cross and the DSO for valour, "much less cooperate with them. It was not that I despised them. I even envied them. But between us was a dark screen of horror and violation; the knowledge of the reality of war. Across that screen I could not communicate. Nor could any of my friends who had the same experience. We could only stand on one side, like exiles in a strange country."

For those who survived, life was precious but evanescent. They were not cavalier, but death was no stranger. They had seen so much that death had no hold on them. In the wake of a war that had betrayed the hopes and dreams of a generation, life mattered less than the moments of being alive.

When we listen today to the voices of these men, be it in poetry, diaries or letters, all part of the cathartic flood of literature that came forth a decade after the armistice, what we hear is the cadence and reserve of a very different kind of man from any we might know or encounter today. Though the madness of what they endured spawned modernity as we know it, they remained scions of another time, a pre-war era so removed from that of our own as to be utterly inaccessible, emotionally, psychologically and spiritually.

And yet, though the Great War ended nearly a century ago, it retains a powerful hold on our imaginations, not just because of the agonies that the conflict inflicted on so many millions of innocent lives. In what Winston Churchill called the blood-stained century of violence, even greater horrors would unfold. What draws us is the character of the men who fought and the values they embodied, traits that we admire to this day, if only because they are so rarely encountered in a culture obsessed with self. These, after all, were men of discretion and decorum, a generation unprepared to litter the world with itself, unwilling to yield feelings to analysis, yet individuals so confident in their masculinity that they could speak of love between men without shame, collect butterflies in the dawn, paint watercolours in late morning, discuss Keats and Shelley over lunch and still be prepared to attack the German lines at dusk. They were men the likes of which we will never know again. Their words and deeds will endure as a testament for the ages. And perhaps for us the most amazing thing of all is that these men were our grandfathers.

NOTE ON SOURCES

Into the Silence: The Great War, Mallory and the Conquest of Everest (Toronto: Knopf Canada, 2011) includes an extended annotated bibliography that references some 600 books as well as much useful and accessible archival material on World War One. Essential for any understanding of what the war implied are two brilliant books: Modris Eksteins, *Rites of Spring: The Great War and the Birth of the Modern Age* (New York: Anchor Books, 1989) and Paul Fussell *The Great War and Modern Memory* (Oxford: Oxford University Press, 1975). For the poets, see Robert Graves, *Good-Bye to All That* (London: Jonathan Cape, 1929); John Stallworthy, *Wilfred Owen* (Oxford: Oxford University Press, 1974); and Max Egremont, *Siegfried Sassoon* (New York: Farrar, Straus and Giroux, 2005). For Geoffrey Winthrop Young, see his books *From the Trenches; Louvain to the Aisne, the First Record of an Eye-Witness* (London: Unwin, 1914) and *The Grace of Forgetting* (London: Country Life Ltd, 1953). For the voice of women, see Vera Brittain, *Testament of Youth* (London: Victor Gollancz, 1934). For the face of battle, see Max Arthur, *Forgotten Voices of the Great War* (Guilford: The Lyons Press, 2002); Laurence Houseman (ed.), *War Letters of Fallen Englishmen*, (London: E. P. Dutton, 1930); Lyn Macdonald (ed.), *1914–1918: Voices and Images of the Great War* (London: Penguin Books, 1991); Martin Middlebrook, *First Day of the Somme* (New York: W. W. Norton, 1972); Anne Powell (ed.), *The Fierce Light* (Aberporth: Palladour Books, 1996); David Robert, *Minds at War: Poetry and Experience of the First World War* (Burgess Hill: Saxon Books, 1996); and two books from Denis Winter: *Death's Men: Soldiers of the Great War* (London: Penguin Books, 1979) and *Haig's Command: A Reassessment* (London: Penguin Books, 1991).

FRANCES ITANI
MESSAGES TO THE LIVING,
MESSAGES TO THE DEAD

THERE IS A FIERCENESS in the air. In and about a quiet area of Belgium and France. In and about pathways and fields, roads of pavement and roads of dust. In and about farms and modest woods that were, at one time, sites of horrific battles at the Western Front.

The fierceness prevails in the smallest graveyards and at the side of towering monuments. It emanates not only from the landscape but from the observer, from the consciousness of those who bear witness, a full century after fighting began.

We can bear witness, long after events have occurred. That is my belief. Details of World War I are still held in the memory of descendants. In the memory of children of soldiers, like my ninety-four-year-old mother, whose father was training in England at the time the war ended in November 1918. My mother's uncle, who served in the artillery throughout the war, wrote home frequently to his younger brother (my grandfather), warning him not to enlist when he came of age. My grandfather did eventually join the war effort and once witnessed the shameful abuse of a horse while training in England. He despised the abuser ever after, and told the story many times in years to come.

Cyril H. Barraud, "The Great Square, Ypres" (detail), circa 1919. Barraud's etching depicts what was left of the town's thirteenth-century Cloth Hall, a victim of four-and-a-half years of almost constant bombardment.

My grandfather's first cousin suffered from a gas attack during the war and returned home to Belleville, Ontario, only to die of lung complications soon afterward. When I think of him, I think of the words of Wilfred Owen from "Dulce et decorum est."

Gas! GAS! Quick, boys! . . .

But someone still was yelling out and stumbling . . .

In all my dreams, before my helpless sight,
He plunges at me, guttering, choking, drowning.

In my version, my grandfather's cousin is the one who is *yelling out and stumbling*. The man I never met, eternally gasping for air, eternally running, not in uniform but in the overalls he'd have worn to the barn every day while he did his chores on the farm at home.

Another of my grandfather's cousins (a young American who came to Canada to enlist) died at the Somme. He was killed four months after he enlisted, possibly during his first battle. His body was never recovered. I found his name on the wall of the Canadian National Vimy Memorial in France. His photograph is in my family album. His descendants, relatives of my own generation, still mourn.

Two of my maternal grandmother's brothers also went off to war. One, referred to as Uncle Jim by the family, began his pilot training at an airfield near Deseronto, Ontario; his younger brother, Uncle Ted, was underage and kept running away to join up. Each time he did so, my great grandmother ran after him and had him released. The third time, she gave up. He enlisted, lying about his age (his war documents, copies of which I now own, attest to this), and fought at the Western Front, saving another of our relatives in the midst of battle by hoisting the wounded man—who had been shot in the knee— over his shoulder and carrying him to safety.

My father's sister told me that one of their older cousins from London, Ontario, had gone to war and come home alive, but had "never been right in the head since." No other information was offered. When I asked for detail, my aunt and my father looked away. It was as if some shameful event had taken place.

In my imagination, these distant and not-so-distant relatives who went off to war are always in motion: digging themselves into trenches; harnessing horses; holding their hands over their ears; hauling and loading the big guns. They swarm, in some sort of otherwise faceless mass, over sodden, eerie land-scapes. I relate the few facts I know about them to my children and grandchildren. Small details that have been retained in my own memory. I was a grandchild who asked questions. Where? And how? And to what end? And why, in the twenty-first century, do I now concern myself with World War I at all?

I ask myself this last question because a disequilibrium exists. A refusal to believe that there was not enough collective will to end the war once it had begun. There is a stubborn refusal on my part to understand how entrenchment was tolerated as the norm while slaughter and sacrifice continued, year after year, with so little ground won by either side.

I was living in Geneva while writing the final pages of my World War I novel *Deafening*. I wrote to my agent,

War flattens me. Some days I can scarcely put pen to paper. I have spent six years researching and writing this novel; I have interviewed veterans of the Great War [some were still alive at the time]; I have read letters, journals, diaries, histories and personal accounts; I have visited battlefields and watched documentaries; I have viewed hundreds of photographs. I have spent an entire summer reading documents in the archives of the Canadian War Museum. Here in Geneva, I've visited the ICRC museum (Musée International de la Croix-Rouge et du Croissant-Rouge) where seven million file cards document prisoners of war and "the missing" from World War I alone. The figures are staggering. I am staggering.

I was falling, had been falling for several years, into an abyss. The fall was not intentional. The abyss was one of awareness.

I read in a report: "We had only 500 casualties today."

I read in a report: "Today 57,000 men were lost."

I read in a report: "We lost three-quarters of our regiment today."

Had the world gone mad? Were the sacrifices essential to the cause? If we think today's world is mad, we need only look back to 1914–1918 to keep things in perspective.

As a writer, I do not turn away. I have taken on a variety of subjects and periods that interest me, and these have included novels, stories, essays and op-ed pieces about World War I. If I have recognized the enormity of the tragedy of this historical period, I have made decisions to impart what I know through journalism and through story. I do not approach the subject by thinking of the nine and a half million people in uniform who died while serving their respective countries. For me, war is about one person, and another, and another, each affected by, each altered by, war. Each having a mother, a father, grand-parents, perhaps a spouse, children, brothers, sisters, aunts, uncles, cousins, friends. Each a social being with a history, a story, many stories, a family "at home." A family like no other family, because it belongs to that one person. The person who has gone "to war."

The characters I create in novels and stories are not abstract, but they could represent many. That is a possibility. The reader decides. John McCrae spoke on behalf of the dead (not long before his own voice was silenced) when he wrote in his iconic poem:

We are the Dead. Short days ago
We lived, felt dawn, saw sunset glow,
   Loved, and were loved . . .

Powerful words that lie below the rim of Canadian conscious-ness, even after all this time. Perhaps McCrae's poem, perhaps art, will outlive all war, all sorrow. Chinua Achebe wrote in *Anthills of the Savannah* that "only the story can continue beyond the war and the warrior. It is the story . . . that saves our progeny from blundering like blind beggars into the spikes of the cactus fence. The story is our escort; without it, we are blind."

IN BELGIUM, there is a museum I wish all Canadians could visit. In Flanders Fields Museum, named after John McCrae's poem, is located in the reconstructed Cloth Hall of Market Square in Ieper (Ypres). This museum, opened in 1998, doubles as a documentation centre, and its collections include five thousand books, trench maps, photographs, original documents and periodicals. Visitors are invited to "touch" the war: to listen, to see historical objects of warfare, to watch audio-visual presentations, to learn about medical care, spiritual welfare _he died. — he had a loving & generous disposition & I knew he would be liked. I know it is a comfort to know he died nobly & for his country still it is a heart break for a mother & we think of them very often & the dear little child. I cannot tell you how much I thank you for all your kindness & for seeing about the burial & I feel so grateful & those kind friends both Officers & men that count with you_ and even personal accounts of Christmas truces. The viewer, the participant, is confronted in material and philosophical ways, all of which point to a contemplation of war and its opposite, peace.

During my two visits to the museum, I heard the words of McCrae read forcefully and aloud, words that drifted through the air, above and around, while visitors examined displays. I heard and read the words of others too. More words from the dead. Lines from Sassoon's poem, "Memorial Tablet": "I died in hell—(They called it Passchendaele)."

The museum contains, in part, what it records as "eye-witness accounts of the Great War":

"At the beginning of the war, when someone was killed . . . we felt it deeply, we went to look. But when we became hardened, we didn't even change direction when he was lying in front of us. We became hard."—*German soldier*

"Then the German behind put his head up again. He was laughing and talking. I saw his teeth glistening against my rifle sight and I pulled the trigger very slowly. He just grunted and crumpled up."—*Captain, 1st Royal Dragoons*

"Sometimes, an infantryman would shoot to the left or the right of me, but I knew the enemy would not use me as a target, despite the light which was as strong as day, because I was Father Christmas, and I was carrying the decorated tree."—*German soldier*

"There was not a sign of life of any sort. . . . Shell hole cut across shell hole . . . slimy mud, mile after mile as far as the eye could see. It is not possible to set down the things that could be written of the Salient. They would haunt your dreams."—*Canadian private*

While I was walking through fields and old trenches and the often muddy landscape of France and Flanders, while pacing around the edge of vast craters, while visiting memorials and cemeteries (the smallest and the largest), while wandering through public and private museums, while staring up at the sky as clouds swept past and the earth seemed to move beneath my feet, I, too, was gathering and creating words. I was thinking of what I wanted to remember and what I wanted to say. I wanted, in some way, to honour the sacrifices that one hundred years ago might have seemed acceptable and unavoidable, though that is not easy to believe today. I experienced a terrible and unrealistic desire to honour every dead soldier; I felt an overwhelming burden to recognize each life taken by that war. But how could this be done in a field that held twelve thousand graves? I tried to notice details on individual stones. The way a maple leaf was carved, a shadow across a marker, an age, a name. And then there were memorials. At Tyne Cot, at the far end of the cemetery, I kept walking and walking around a large semicircular wall, trying to get past the carved names of 34,857 men who had fallen in the Ypres Salient and whose graves are still unknown. How could this many men, lost in the soil, be imagined?

I wanted to ask questions of the dead. I wanted to say, Were you frightened? How did you push down your fear?

I wanted to say to each of the soldiers buried under soil and clay, I am trying to remember for you, because your life was important.

I visited battlefields and knew I could never write enough,

remember enough, be present enough.

I wanted to say, Life goes on, but your war is still present.

Indeed, the war is part of everyday life in rural areas of France and Belgium, even in the twenty-first century. Farmers work their fields in ordinary ways, while tons of World War I debris are coughed up out of the soil each year. Yes, tons. Difficult to believe. I was travelling with another writer—a friend from Alberta—and we were driven by our English friend and guide, Bruce, who pointed out the evidence, heaped along the edges of country roads. Farmers stack war debris, shrapnel, pieces of metal, digging tools, badges, rusted bayonets, canteens, iron wheels, old wire, all of this awaiting pickup by collectors whose job it is to drive along the roads periodically and haul it away.

Occasionally, a large unexploded shell will surface. This happened at one of the Canadian sites in France just before I visited. The area had been roped off, and French *démineurs* had promised to come soon to remove the shell. But not all incidents end well. In March 2014, the *Ottawa Citizen* reported that an armament from World War I had exploded at an industrial site in the former Flanders battlegrounds. Two construction workers were killed and two were wounded. The cause was reported as "a shell or grenade." "Most armaments that surface," the article continued, "are destroyed without incident by an army bomb squad."

ONE OF THE PLACES at which I stayed when I was in Belgium was a château, a timbered structure called Kasteelhof 't Hooghe. Outside the grounds is the Menin Road. Within the property, uneven landscape, gardens, a giant willow tree, a small lake which is, in fact, an old crater—an historic crater—that over time has filled naturally with water. The entire property is directly on the old front line. The château is a venerable-looking building with trailing vines and a complicated series of angled rooftops and double chimneys. The windows of my second-storey room were hinge-locked, and a hinge-locked door led to a narrow balcony. To open either the windows or the balcony door, I had to pull down on a levered handle, a slow-motion action that was somewhat like drawing down a long iron switch. From my balcony, I could look out through branches and leaves towards the deep crater below. When I turned off the light, my room fell into sudden blackness. Not a glimmer anywhere.

When I'd first arrived, a young man who worked at the château had provided me with a one-sheet history in English, outlining the fighting that had taken place on the grounds. The château had at one time been owned by the Baron de Vinck. Between 1914 and 1918, the property changed hands many times, back and forth between British and German troops. Tunnelling companies exploded several underground mines during this period. In 1915, one British explosion left a crater sixteen metres deep and forty metres wide.

But the Germans recaptured the crater and adjacent trenches. And then, at a cost of four thousand casualties, a British attack failed to retake the same ground again. Mines were exploded by German troops throughout the Hooge area. The property continued to change hands until, finally, in 1918, Hooge was captured for the last time by the British.

Eventually, the large crater became the present-day lake.

The young man who gave me the printed history worked and lived at the château alongside his parents. He told me there was

Sanctuary Wood, Ypres, Belgium, 2014.

a tank at the bottom of the lake. At the end of the war, he said, local people had been trying to clear their fields, and they had pushed the heavy vehicle down into the crater. He added that a Canadian dugout that could hold as many as thirty soldiers had recently been found just down the road, in a local brickyard.

Even a hundred years later, reminders of those four deadly years continue to surface. In cabinets with glass doors, and along ledges and sills on the first floor of the château, artifacts of war are displayed: knives, bullets, buttons, badges, shrapnel. I was told that a body once drifted up to the surface of the lake. Immediately, I thought, Bones? Fragments of uniform? How would these have resembled a body? And how many more bodies still lie at the bottom of the crater?

During dinner at the château, the young man carried a book to our table. Mainly photographs, Flemish text. He pointed out photos of the family property. While leafing through the pages, I became aware of violent winds blowing outside. Gale-force winds. I thought of earlier weathers endured. I thought of the dead, so close, so buried, so smothered, so lost.

Upstairs, the windows shuddered and shook throughout the night. No one in the building slept easily. In the morning, I looked out and saw that the giant willow tree outside my window had fallen. Even on its side, its shaggy branches reached up to the panes of glass on the second floor. Two men were already at work, sawing the tree into chunks. They would struggle for days trying to break this enormous tree into carrying-size pieces. A third man was on the roof, having climbed to the top of one of the double chimneys by a series of five ladders. He was removing parts of the chimney as well as red tiles that had broken or become loose during the gale. I walked outside before breakfast and wandered around the base of the tree so that I could examine its roots. I wondered if more war debris had been uprooted and exposed. At breakfast, I was told that most of the war souvenirs in the glass cabinets had been dug from the garden. "We have to dig down at least a metre," the waiter said, "before we find bones and uniforms."

After leaving the château that morning, I walked along the road to the Hooge Crater Cemetery. The following graves are here: 5,182 British, 105 Canadian, 513 Austrian, 121 New Zealand, 2 British West Indian. Almost 3,600 of those buried are not identified by name.

Our guide, Bruce, arrived at the cemetery to collect me, and we drove on to what was perhaps the quietest place I was to visit in Belgium: Essex Farm Cemetery and ADS (Advanced Dressing Station).

No one else was there when we arrived, and I was able to enter one of the bunker-like rooms where John McCrae had looked after wounded and dying men. I sat in a small, squared space and contemplated his work. At the time he was there, the atmosphere would not have been so peaceful.

THERE WERE STILL PLACES to visit. Bruce drove up Canadalaan, which is lined with Canadian maples, and brought us to Hill 62 and a private section of Sanctuary Wood. I wandered slowly along trenches that zigzagged through trees and returned by way of a small on-site museum.

If ever I have seen images that might be able to stop war for all time, it was inside this private museum. Twelve wooden viewing boxes contained stereoscopic views of hundreds of photographs taken during and immediately following the Great War. I stayed for some time, inspecting photos, moving from one viewing box to the next. Two of the views will stay with me forever.

In the first: barren, muddy landscape containing one tall and leafless tree. A full horse's head and two long legs with hoofs have been blasted upward and droop over the branches of the tree. The remainder of this huge animal's body is missing.

In the second photo: a soldier's body is draped in a V over the branch of another dead tree. The soldier's head is missing.

I stared at these photos. If only, I thought. If only these could be seen by persons who make decisions to wage war, and by those who send others to war. If only these could be seen by those who enlist in wars, and who finance war behind the scenes. If only images and words could be powerful enough. And though the human condition has always included war, we, as artists, must not give up reflecting what armed hostility truly means—using images and photographs and all other forms of art. Using words.

In *Deafening*, I wrote, "War churned on as the earth circled the sun. Reliable and grim, it continued to swallow hundreds, thousands, hundreds of thousands of young men."

In my novel *Tell*, the young soldier Kenan, who returns to Canada shell-shocked and damaged, says, "All I want now is to let out the dangerous words that are in my head. I can't say them, in or out of the house. I can't set things right. What happened over there. How could anything that comes from war ever be set right?"

Kenan's question has no answer. His words, and sentiments similar to his, are echoed by the many visitors who continue to visit the battlefields of the Western Front.

DURING OUR FINAL EVENING in Belgium, we visited the Menin Gate, where every night at 8 p.m. a brief ceremony is held. Two policemen pulled up in a van. They got out, and one stopped traffic in both directions. The other policeman led children who were on bicycles to the side of the road, where they would be able to witness a nightly ritual that has gone on since 1927, with interruptions only during the Second World War. From the small crowd that gathered—students, cadets, visitors—two buglers stepped forward and began to play the "Last Post" in perfect harmony. The crowd listened in silence. The Menin Gate bears the names of almost 55,000 soldiers who died in Belgium and whose graves are not known. I stood beneath the inscribed names of 6,994 Canadians who are part of this tragic number.

Minutes later, traffic resumed. The cadets marched away. I turned to the side and saw small candles burning along the ledges of the huge monument. There were poppies, too, placed among brief notes and scraps of paper attached to tiny wooden crosses. These scraps of paper contained messages to the dead. One of them read, "You have done miricals for us." Another was a Canadian message: "From the one daughter of your baby sister."

No miracle has stopped war. Many of us do still remember.

Overleaf: A.Y. Jackson, "A Copse, Evening," 1918. While other members of the Group of Seven produced war art, Jackson was the only member to enlist as a soldier. He was wounded near Ypres in 1916.

SCYLLA AND YBDIS.

I don't say it in any simply to show you in the country. I he other evening in

distressingly bored, nwards on the floor. g the hands of the the ancients had it, her.

not the signal for a

James," said Lillah, while Phyllis said

the way to rouse

babies," I said. had died down they at be of some use. he War," said Lillah. hyllis.

began, "is a very

Mummie says," said of reproach. aving pilfered some-

ays," added Lillah, , "it's a disgrace to

mmme, he wishes he," said Phyllis with

illah went on, "that the flag. Are we?" nswered. s want our flag?" rything."

we give them one Phyllis with deadly

an't even keep their

nd it to the wash,"

o to," I answered

o are fighting for Are we?" I said, "is always

Phyllis gravely. "I knew." lso," I said with n wrong." derous silence. Daddy," said Lillah, ver very bright." aid I. I shall say a Margaret about that nto the children's

e won," said Phyllis, visation?"

"What will it be like—a fairy-tale?"
"Very probably."
"Daddy says it's freedom. What's freedom?"
"Freedom," I said "is—er—being able to do what you like."
"Then won't there be any policemen after the War?"
"Oh yes, we shall keep the policemen."
"Why?"
"Because the streets would look so bare without them."
They looked at me with suspicion; even at that tender age they could not believe in an æsthetic ratepayer.
"Do people like the War?" said Phyllis.
"No," I answered. That was easy.
"Not even the Germans?"
"I think not."
"But if nobody made the big guns there wouldn't be any war?"
"Er—no," I said.
"Then why do people——?"
"Well—er——" I stopped. I could see that my last rags of reputation for brightness were going. I was in the Uncle's last ditch.
"When you are older," I began; but Lillah interrupted.
"And why don't policemen take the people who make the guns?" It was Phyllis's shot.
"And if nobody wants the War what makes it go on?"
"And if it's a disgrace," queried Lillah, "why does Daddy want to go?"
"And why," began Phyllis; but I put up my hand.
"One day," I said, "I must tell you the story of Socrates, who had to drink a very nasty medicine called hemlock."
"What for?" said Lillah.
"For asking too many questions," I said.
"Were the people who gave it to him the people who didn't know the answers?" said Lillah.
"Yes, they were," I said, as I rose. I took out my watch.
"Good heavens, it's after bedtime!"
"Does your watch say right?" said Phyllis.
"It sometimes underestimates, but it never exaggerates," I said. At that moment Daddy himself appeared.
"Good-night chicks," he said. "Has Uncle James been amusing you?"
"We've been playing with him," said Lillah with gravity.
And if ever there was a *double entendre* I'll swear it was there. And so they went to bed.
"I don't know," I said to George as we went downstairs, "why you called your daughters Lillah and Phyllis; their real names are Scylla and Charybdis."

But George is a dull man, and simply said that Charybdis Watson would have sounded ridiculous.

SEASONABLE (?) NOVELTIES.

A catalogue of Christmas toys contains a Mechanical Motor-accident and a Realistic Trench-warfare model, "with apparatus for Poison-Gas." Surely this method of preventing children's minds from dwelling upon the cheery side of life is capable of further extension, as under:—

The Frozen-pipe Doll's House.—Charmingly-furnished six-room House, with complete model system of Leaking Pipes. Real Water can be made to run down the walls. Paper peels off, etc. Endless Fun for Young and Old. 7s. 6d. and 10s. 6d.

Larger, with workable Kitchen-boiler Explosion, and death of Cook. 15s.

The Influenza Doll.—Exquisite model, with hand-painted Red Nose, dressed in real blankets. On be ng squeezed the Doll emits a cough similar to that produced by severe bronchial congestion. 6s.

Superior quality, with Double-Pneumonia effect. 8s. 6d.

Elegant Model Cinema Theatre, with Igniting Film and real Flames. Just the toy for a Thoughtful Child. Complete in box, with four refills of combustible Model Audience. 21s.

The Little Dentist.—Entire outfit, including miniature Forceps, Gags, Gasbags, etc. Will keep an entire Nursery happy for hours. Help Baby with his Teething. 5s. 6d. the set (or, including model Electric-drill and old Illustrated Papers for Waiting-room, 12s.).

IN FLANDERS FIELDS.

In Flanders fields the poppies blow
Between the crosses, row on row,
　That mark our place; and in the sky
　The larks, still bravely singing, fly
Scarce heard amid the guns below.

We are the Dead. Short days ago
We lived, felt dawn, saw sunset glow,
　Loved and were loved, and now we lie
　　In Flanders fields.

Take up our quarrel with the foe:
To you from failing hands we throw
　The torch; be yours to hold it high.
　If ye break faith with us who die
We shall not sleep, though poppies grow
　　In Flanders fields.

"Will this war bring us to Kidderminster?"
English Churchman.

Well, there are worse places than Kidderminster.

JONATHAN VANCE
A MOMENT'S PERFECTION

AS HE CASUALLY SHOVED the piece of paper into his pocket, John McCrae had no inkling that the fifteen lines he had written would catapult him to international fame. "In Flanders Fields" was, to him, more cathartic than anything, written to help him come to terms with all he had seen and experienced over the past few weeks. While it was deeply personal, even therapeutic, for him, the poem would catch the spirit of the English-speaking world and become an anthem for a generation. Long after McCrae's death, it remains one of the most recognizable elements of the cultural legacy of the First World War.

McCrae may not have written "In Flanders Fields" with publication in mind, but, perhaps on the advice of some close friends, he tinkered with it over the summer of 1915 in the hope of placing it with a reputable journal. It finally appeared in Punch magazine, unsigned, in the December 8, 1915, issue (its author was identified in the annual index), printed in a way that made it look entirely unremarkable. Its North American debut came in the Washington Post in January 1916, and from there it quickly spread. By the end of February, it had appeared in newspapers in Atlanta, Georgia; Hamilton, Australia; and even tiny Parsons, Kansas; but not yet in Canada. It appeared in the Vancouver Daily World in March; unlike almost every other paper,

Punch magazine, December 1915. "In Flanders Fields" (uncredited, bottom right) makes a humble debut.

the *Daily World* identified John McCrae as the author. Over the summer of 1916 and through 1917, the poem was reprinted in publications as diverse as the *Citizen* of Berea, Kentucky; Australia's *West Gippsland Gazette*; and the *New Zealand Herald*. By the time the Toronto *Globe* printed it in September 1917, in a tastefully decorated display box, it was already a sensation.

According to McCrae's Montreal colleague and fellow writer Andrew Macphail, "In Flanders Fields" gave "expression to a mood which at the time was universal, and will remain as a permanent record when the mood is passed away." Stylistically, its imagery called to mind the nature poetry of the Victorian era, as well as Canada's Confederation poets, such as Wilfred Campbell and Frederick George Scott. Its meter, straight-forward diction and simple rhyme scheme made it easy to memorize and perfect for recitation. The sentiment underlying it—profound sadness but a firm conviction in the rightness of the cause and in the willing-ness of the living to continue the struggle—connected deeply with societies that had lost so much and would undoubtedly be called upon to give even more before the war was won. The poem also spread so rapidly, it must be admitted, because of the absence of any meaningful copyright protection. As a Canadian who had published in an English magazine, McCrae occupied a grey area in copyright terms, and there was little anyone could do to prevent the poem from being reproduced in any context, for any purpose. Over the years, "In Flanders Fields" would be used to generate support and money for all kinds of causes, good and bad; McCrae had no control over these uses, nor did he see a penny of the money that was made.

It seems unlikely that McCrae was particularly bothered when the poem was mobilized for partisan political purposes in Canada, assuming that the politics involved winning the war, but he may have been less pleased with the poem's use for commercial purposes. Before the war, he had been a medical examiner for a number of Boston insurance carriers. In 1917, some of the insurance men commissioned composer Charles Ives to set the poem to music as an ornament to their annual sales convention. Would McCrae have been happy to know that "In Flanders Fields" graced an advertisement for Brill Brothers men's clothiers in New York when the base commercialism was softened by the claim that ten cents of every dollar spent would go to the American Red Cross War Fund? If McCrae was bothered by commercial uses of his poem, he didn't let on. He did, however, comment wryly on the inability of many people in the newspaper industry to spell his name correctly. He was silent on the fact that the title and occasionally lines of the poem itself were also frequently rendered incorrectly.

By early 1918, "In Flanders Fields" had already taken the English-speaking world by storm, and it was about to be elevated to a different level entirely. McCrae's death from pneumonia in January 1918 added another poignant layer of meaning to the poem. With the fallen robbed of the voice that spoke most eloquently for them (assuming one doubted the woman from Roland, Manitoba, who told a Winnipeg newspaper that she was receiving poetry from John McCrae from beyond the grave), others came forward to carry the poetic torch, to ensure that McCrae's injunction to the living survived his death. From established writers, including publisher and cartoonist John Wilson Bengough and Charles W. Gordon (better known as the novelist Ralph Connor), to poets who wisely elected to remain anonymous, they created a body of verse so substantial that it might constitute a separate sub-genre: replies to "In Flanders Fields."

As poetry, these efforts amount to little, but they do affirm the impact of the original poem. Written at a time when the future was very much hanging in the balance, they replace the nagging doubt over the war's ultimate outcome with a sense of absolute certainty: we *will* hold the torch; we *will* keep the faith. The consequences of not doing so, as Blyth Wood predicted in "The Torch-Bearers," were dire:

If we break faith with them, the loyal dead,
    The torch within our grasp with dying flame,
Above our downcast eyes and drooping head,
    A smoking brand, our guilt shall wide proclaim.

But the responses were not just Canadian, for "In Flanders Fields" was every bit as popular throughout the British Empire and in the United States. American amateur poets offered countless replies, such as R.W. Lilliard's "America's Answer," which appeared in the *New York Evening Post* shortly after McCrae's death.

Rest ye in peace, ye Flanders dead.
The fight that ye so bravely led
We've taken up. And we will keep
True faith with you who lie asleep
With each a cross to mark his bed,
And poppies blowing overhead,
Where once his own lifeblood ran red.
So let your rest be sweet and deep
    In Flanders fields.

Fear not that ye have died for naught.
The torch ye threw to us is caught.
Ten million hands will hold it high,
And Freedom's light shall never die.
We've learned the lesson that ye taught
    In Flanders fields.

Less accomplished but equally acclaimed, if only because its author was a prominent politician, was "In Flanders Fields" by Missouri senator Mark McGruder, who wrote to the Toronto *Globe* that McCrae's verse "has created more favorable comment than any wartime poem written thus far." In his response, the senator attempted to capture "the feeling of our people toward those brave Canadians who have died that the world might be safe for democracy."

The replies were only one element of the explosion of interest in "In Flanders Fields" after McCrae's death, when the poem became an even more powerful tool for promoting patriotic causes. In Canada's Victory Loans campaign of 1919, the final stanza was excerpted as "The Call," and was followed by an anonymous verse entitled "The Answer," carrying the message that Canadians had to get down to work and prepare to win the battle of the peace. At the same time, a leaflet produced by Canada's food controller announced, "Help Our Farmers to Produce Food—Do Not Break Faith!" In Australia, advertisers employed the poem to encourage people to purchase war savings certificates, and it provided the theme for a widely published letter in favour of conscription. It was a centrepiece of the American Red Cross Society's campaign to raise $100 million and was also heavily used in the Third Liberty Loan campaign. "That little poem, just fifteen lines in length,"

Peace rules the Day, where Wisdom rules the Mind.

Collins

In Flanders' Fields

In Flanders' fields the poppies blow
  Between the crosses row on row,
That mark our place, and in the sky
  The larks still bravely singing fly,
Scarce heard amid the guns below.

We are the dead. Short days ago
  We lived, felt dawn, saw sunset glow,
Loved and were loved, and now we lie
  In Flanders' fields.

McCRAE

observed the *Globe*, "has done more for the civilian morale of this country than any other written or spoken contribution to the cause: and its influence promises to be equally potent south of the line."

The end of the war in November 1918 affirmed that the torch had been held, the faith kept—the fallen could sleep, for the living had finished the job they had started. With the weight of uncertainty lifted, it was time to reflect on the poem and its author. Humorist and McGill University economist Stephen Leacock wrote a fond and touching appreciation in the *Times* (London) that recalled McCrae's years in Company K (the University of Toronto company of the Queen's Own Rifles, the militia regiment in which McCrae had served as a student). The company had always been the butt of undergraduate humour, "but looking back upon them in retrospect," Leacock wrote wistfully, "they appear a band of heroes. McCrae's name is only one of an honoured list of Canadian soldiers, dead and living, whose first service to their country was in the drill squad of Company K." The first collection of McCrae's verse, *In Flanders Fields and Other Poems*, appeared in 1920, with poems dating back to 1894 and including "An Essay in Character" by Andrew Macphail. Part literary criticism, part biography and part reminiscence, Macphail's essay is a moving reflection on a poem that captured millions of hearts and on the poet who left an equally deep impression on those who knew him best. Aggressively advertised by Ryerson Press, its Toronto publisher, the book immediately shot to the top of the bestseller list.

An abbreviated version of "In Flanders Fields" on a greeting card produced in the early 1920s; illustrator unknown.

The literary critics were virtually unanimous—leaving aside the qualified praise of Ryerson publisher Lorne Pierce (he ventured that McCrae would have changed the line "Take up our quarrel with the foe" if he'd had the chance). They could scarcely find an adjective sufficient to describe the poem's brilliance. Archibald MacMechan, who wrote one of the first critical assessments of Canadian literature, did not believe there was much in the national canon that would hold up in the future. He predicted that snippets of work by Leacock, Archibald Lampman and Marjorie Pickthall might be salvaged for various collections but that the most notable and enduring contribution was certainly "McCrae's perfect rondeau." The *New York Times* ranked it as one of the three pre-eminent poems of the war, along with Rupert Brooke's "The Soldier" and Alan Seeger's "I Have a Rendezvous with Death," calling it "a poem that embodied in verse, the white hot ideals of a man with whom literature was not a vocation but an avocation." "A perfect job," declared the newspaper. The *Brisbane Courier* in Australia called it "probably the most poignant and enduring of all the poems of the Great War," while the *Northern Champion* in Taree, New South Wales, praised McCrae's "genuine poetic gift." Ontario Agricultural College literature professor O.J. Stevenson, in a book of short sketches of prominent Canadian authors and artists, gave McCrae pride of place as the very first entry. Visiting McCrae's grave at Wimereux Cemetery in 1922, Stevenson recalled that "it had been theirs to hold high the torch of freedom—and as we turned to look back at Wimereux, remembering their sacrifice it seemed to us that 'The very graves were for a moment bright.'" In the midst of the Second World War, E.K. Brown judged "In Flanders Fields" to be a "masterpiece . . . where careful art, studied moderation in tone, and intense as well as perfectly represented emotion fused to produce a moment's perfection." It was hardly surprising that the poem appeared in virtually every anthology of Canadian poetry published in the postwar decades.

The poem's literary merit was secondary to its meaning, however, for it had already become a central element in how Canadians understood and remembered the war. Its very phrases—keeping the faith and holding the torch—had entered the vernacular as shorthand for duty and obligation. When Andrew Macphail wrote that the fallen had "observed the rows of crosses lengthen, the torch thrown, caught, and carried to victory," he was referring specifically to the Allied victory in November 1918. "The dead may sleep," he concluded. "We have not broken faith with them."

But in the following years, "In Flanders Fields" was not connected solely to the First World War. It now referred to the peacetime battles to build a better world and keep it safe from future war. Surely McCrae had not imagined, wrote an Australian editor, that patriotism was unnecessary after the war was won; on the contrary, it was essential to continue fighting against what Germany had stood for: "the foe in our midst in the form of materialism, selfishness, shams, disease and poverty." It was, in short, a lesson for the coming generations. As the Reverend R.G. MacBeth, of First Presbyterian Church in Vancouver, wrote, the poem had "won a hundred battles, inspired the Allies to new endeavour in the hours of crisis and made slacking impossible to men and nations whose souls were sufficiently alive to understand the passionate appeal of the Anxious Dead. . . . We could wish nothing better for all young Canadians than that the spirit and power in which John McCrae lived and died in the great conflict for freedom should be one of their prized possessions." For the Reverend H.T. Gornall, a Nova Scotia clergyman who volunteered for service as a chaplain during the First World War, speaking at the dedication of Yarmouth's war memorial in 1923, McCrae's torch was the torch of liberty: "May it be ours to hold high and wave the torch until all the world shall rally to the cause of patriotism and right." The Episcopal bishop of New York, William T. Manning, called it "the poem of all those who understand the meaning of the great conflict and of the sacrifice made by those who gave themselves for the right. It is the voice of the dear dead calling on us who live to see that their sacrifice shall not have been made in vain." As poet Eugene Standerwick put it, "The men and women who fought for peace, are fighting still by carrying on the torch from the hands no longer able to tread the road of life."

"In Flanders Fields" was omnipresent in manifestations of the memory of the war, not just in Canada but around the Allied world. It was a standard text at the dedications of war memorials and military cemeteries, and it also inspired many memorials. One of the more popular designs, created by sculptor Emanuel Hahn and sold by Toronto's Thomson Monument Company, was a resting soldier gazing wistfully at a battlefield cross inscribed with the words "In Flanders Fields." In New Zealand, one correspondent suggested for her local memorial a granite tomb surmounted by an athletic young figure captured in the act of "flinging the torch." More often, the poem was echoed by the inclusion of a torch in the decorative stonework of the monument. For decades, newspaper editorials appearing around Armistice Day and Remembrance Day, or Poppy Day in the United States, pondered whether, over the previous year, the torch had been held, the faith kept. Veterans' organizations used it as the theme for parade floats, and it was a staple of Anzac Day observances in Australia and New Zealand. During Auckland's Peace Festival in 1919, one business decorated its window with a representation of an old trench flanked by graves and poppies, a tableau inspired by an illustrated version of "In Flanders Fields" that had appeared in the *Ladies' Home Journal*. When the Canadian government was producing its official First World War film and the subject of titles came up, "They Kept the Faith" and "Flanders Fields" were popular suggestions. And in 1922, when the American Battle Monuments Commission proposed using headstones instead of crosses on American military graves in Europe, one veteran pleaded with the commission's chair, General of the Armies John J. Pershing, to reverse the decision by imagining how McCrae's verse would sound if it were rewritten "In Flanders fields the poppies grow / Between the squat little headstones, row on row."

But for all the high ideals the poem represented, its very ubiquity cheapened it. As it ceased to belong to Canada or even to the First World War and was adopted by anyone and anything, it came to be used for all sorts of purposes that were unconnected to McCrae's original message. Woodrow Wilson used it in 1920 to predict victory for the Democrats in the upcoming presidential election. That same year, it was quoted in connection with the opening of the Australian football season. In New Zealand, a writer cited it in a letter protesting archaeological research on ancient Maori burial sites. In 1925, the patriotic organization Young America mobilized the poem in its call to the nation to resist "Ultra-Progressivism, Socialism, Communism or Bolshevism . . . foreign-conceived Demagoguery [and] the deluded, deceiving deliriums of Lenin and Trotsky and their disciples." In July 1940, American-born Nazi propagandist

Fred Kaltenbach read it during a radio broadcast from Berlin that urged the United States to stay out of the war if it wanted to avoid the prospect of countless young Americans joining the ranks of those sleeping in Flanders fields. A horse named Flanders Fields ran at Toronto's Woodbine Raceway in the early 1940s; fittingly, he sired a foal named Ceasefire. And for decades, commercial enterprises such as Saks & Company of New York and the Jack Lyons Chop House trotted out "In Flanders Fields" for advertising purposes; the fact that they did so on Remembrance Day hardly made it any less tasteless. Its use in an advertisement by a manufacturer of surgical dressings might be regarded as particularly inappropriate.

By 1939, the poem had been enlisted for its second war. This one would be much bigger, costlier and more destructive than either of McCrae's wars, the Second Boer War and the First World War, and as a medical man he would have marvelled at our ability to come up with new ways to destroy the human body. The 1940s was a decidedly less poetic era than the 1910s; young people no longer wrote poetry as a matter of course, and newspaper columns were no longer filled with amateur poems on any conceivable subject. Because writing verse now seemed a little old-fashioned, the Second World War spawned far less poetry than the First, which meant that there was little to challenge the status of "In Flanders Fields" as the most revered war poem of the century. Only John Gillespie Magee's "High Flight" even approached it in popularity, and when the Toronto *Globe* pronounced Earle Birney's "On Going to the Wars" as "the great Canadian poem of the war," the benchmark it used was "In Flanders Fields." The *Townsville Daily Bulletin* in Australia declared that it was "the greatest poem of that war . . . with a message to each and every one of us, the fathers, brothers, sons

An ad for surgical dressings featuring Philip Lyford's painting
"Flanders Fields," *Ladies Home Journal*, 1918.

and friends of those who did not fear to die for God and country, and for us, the living." The *New Zealand Herald* called it "the poem that most caught the popular mind, and that still to-day has a chief place in the public affection." Two decades after his death, John McCrae remained the war poet for a new generation.

One can only be struck by how easily the quintessential poem of the First World War was mobilized for the Second. Neither its diction nor its sentiment was anything less than completely relevant to the new challenges. Indeed, it came to symbolize the fundamental continuity between the two wars. In Australia, patriotic events often featured a "passing the torch" ceremony. At a Win the War Rally in 1940 in the town of Nambour, Queensland, the oldest local veteran of the First World War passed a torch to the youngest soldier from the area while the master of ceremonies recited "In Flanders Fields." "If we accept anything less than complete victory in this war," said Australia's deputy director of recruiting during a drive for volunteers in 1941, "we will be breaking faith with the men who sleep in Flanders fields, in the Libyan desert, on Mount Olympus, and in Crete, Syria, and the blue waters of the Mediterranean."

And so, once again, "In Flanders Fields" was a staple in advertising for Victory Bond campaigns (or Liberty Loan drives, as they were known in the United States and Australia), fund-raising drives, memorial services and patriotic speeches. In August 1940, Prime Minister Mackenzie King travelled to Ogdensburg, New York, to meet with President Franklin Delano Roosevelt to conclude an agreement for financing the war. One of the supporting events was a memorial service for members of the 28th Division, Pennsylvania National Guard, who had been killed in the First World War, and an American clergyman read "In Flanders Fields" as part of the program. In a federal by-election campaign in February 1942, Ontario premier Mitchell Hepburn quoted McCrae in a speech urging the voters of Welland to reject the Liberal candidate, federal labour minister Humphrey Mitchell. The poem continued to find favour with literary anthologists and editors of verse collections such as Ryerson Press's *Flying Colours* (1942), edited by Charles G.D. Roberts, himself a veteran of the First World War and a poet of McCrae's generation. And when the Ontario education ministry contemplated removing "In Flanders Fields" from school textbooks, the plan was widely excoriated, provincial Conservative leader George Drew castigating the government for imagining that it could take away such a "patriotic gem" from Ontario schoolchildren.

In the wake of the Second World War, the co-opting of "In Flanders Fields" continued. Because it was so well known, it seemed to be at the fingertips of anyone who had a cause to promote. At various times, McCrae's verse was presented as part of an argument to preserve the Armouries on Toronto's University Avenue from the wrecker's ball; to retain capital punishment; to reject Lester Pearson's design for a new Canadian flag; to pressure motion picture studios into making more Canadian war films; and to reopen negotiations regarding French fishing rights around the islands of Saint-Pierre and Miquelon. But it wasn't just in Canada that "In Flanders Fields" remained an all-purpose metaphor. In Canberra, Australia, another horse named Flanders Fields contested the turf. In 1963, the president of Eastern Oregon College quoted it in a tribute to recently assassinated John F. Kennedy. More than three decades later, an American senator used it to urge the House Judiciary Committee to impeach President Bill Clinton. It came up in a letter to the editor from a California anti-abortionist and in an interview with a football coach about the injuries his team had suffered on the field. And what better way to describe the respect for the traditions of the University of North Carolina than by reference to "the great war poem, 'In Flanders Fields.' 'Be ours the torch to hold it high,' and we feel that we cannot break faith with those who have been here before us."

Beginning in the late 1950s, critics began to turn against the poem. This was partly because, in an era when modernist verse was finally gaining wide acceptance, "In Flanders Fields" now seemed even more dated, but it was also a consequence of the broader cultural turn against the idealism and principles of the First World War. A series of enormously popular works—books such as Leon Wolff's *In Flanders Fields: The 1917 Campaign* (1958) and Alan Clark's *The Donkeys: A History of the British Expeditionary Force in 1915* (1961), the stage play *Oh What a Lovely War* (1963), Stanley Kubrick's film *Paths of Glory* (1957)—painted a picture of the Great War as a foolish exercise in national self-mutilation in which credulous youths were fed tales of glory and self-sacrifice to camouflage the brutality, stupidity and selfishness of pointless violence. In this new orthodoxy, McCrae was portrayed as a cheerleader, one of the older generation "speeding glum heroes up the line to death." The patriotism of his poem was reinterpreted as a prime example of the most pernicious kind of jingoism. Literary critic Paul Fussell, in his enormously influential *The Great War and Modern Memory* (1975), averred that, in judging the poem, words such as "'vicious' and 'stupid' would not seem to go too far." Jon Silkin included it very reluctantly in his *Penguin Book of First World War Poetry* (1979), not because he was convinced of its literary merit but because readers would expect to see it in such a collection. A generation later, Canadian poet Nancy Holmes admitted that it was "a rather assured little word machine" whose first two stanzas were "marvels of artful construction" but concluded that the last six lines brought "a disappointment so acute that it erases the sympathetic reading of the first nine lines." Margaret Atwood, editor of *The New Oxford Book of Canadian Verse in English* (1982), admitted that the poem had been "hammered into [her] head at an early age," leaving the reader to assume that she sympathized with Silkin's decision. Indeed, hers is one of the few recent literary anthologies to include "In Flanders Fields." The fact that it was later politicized by conservative (and Conservative) political figures has only damned it further in some eyes.

And yet the general public has never been especially interested in the views of literary critics. They don't particularly care if the poem's rhyme scheme is facile or its imagery Victorian, and they're not swayed by the uses and abuses of McCrae's work after his death. The critical turn against the poem is virtually the only thing that has changed about it. In the twenty-first century, it continues to be used just as it was throughout the twentieth—recited by schoolchildren at assemblies, read solemnly to crowds at Remembrance, Memorial or Anzac Day, exploited by advertisers and bandied about on behalf of every imaginable cause. The fact that "In Flanders Fields" has long been politicized, commercialized and commodified does not compromise its powerful imagery and genuine sentiment. People continue to see it, one hopes, exactly as McCrae wrote it a century ago: as an ode to a generation who gave their best to preserve ideals that, to them, meant everything.

NOTE ON SOURCES

Many of the sources used for this chapter are taken from scrapbooks kept by the McCrae family (primarily, it seems, by David McCrae) and kept in McCrae House, in Guelph, Ontario. The author is happy to supply specific references on request.

THAT MARK OUR PLACE

Above: Burial ground, the Somme, date unknown.

Opposite: Ypres, 1915. The makeshift graves of three privates from the Princess Patricia's Canadian Light Infantry. Their remains were later moved to the Ypres Reservoir Cemetary, Belgium.

Vimy Ridge, 1918.

Thelus, 1918.

Aux Rietz Corner, 1918.

The Somme, 1916.

Ypres, 1917.

Vimy Ridge, 1918.

Arras, 1918.

Étaples, 1918.

Vimy Station, 1917.

Above: Newfoundland Memorial Park, Beaumont-Hamel, France, 1925.

Opposite: The Canadian National Vimy Memorial, photographed by Flight Lieutenant Alex Gray in August 1944, shortly after the liberation of France. The photo was intended to show that retreating German forces had not destroyed or damaged the Monument.

JOSEPH BOYDEN
THREE TOURS OF FLANDERS

SUMMER 2005 My son, Jacob, and I bicycle along a rural
Belgian road. The July sun shines and the breeze causes the
fields to undulate in green and golden waves. He's just turned
fifteen and has a metal detector strapped on his back. We pedal
along an area called the Ypres Salient, this landscape not all
that different from Southern Ontario's. Neither of us speaks
French or Flemish or Dutch or German, but Jacob swooned
over the waitresses in the square the evening before, who
seemed to fluently speak all of these languages, and I was
grateful when they didn't balk at Jacob ordering a beer.

My first novel had just come out and had done well enough
that I could afford to bring my boy and my wife, Amanda, and
my dear friend Jim Steel, the man who'd been invaluable to the
novel's research, over for a trip to this part of Europe. I thought
I'd been done writing about the Great War.

Two days before our outing, Jacob suffered through a fit of
screaming, a meltdown that became self-harming and caused
the hotel's security to knock on our door and threaten to evict
us. Amanda and I wondered aloud if we'd all have to fly home
after having just arrived.

We bicycle on this July day looking for souvenirs in farmers'
fields. Some of the most brutal fighting the world has ever seen
happened right here ninety years before, and every year since,

A Canadian soldier carries his transport, 1917, location unknown.

the earth continues to push up its proof from the depths. Bullets and shrapnel balls, pieces of helmets, rusted rifle barrels, unexploded 18-pounder shells, uniform buttons and canteens and buckles, the odd femur or skull.

Jacob and I stop at a field enclosed by a chest-high wire fence. We lean our bikes on it and examine the surroundings. A hill in the distance rises just a mortar's arc away, the acres in front of us growing corn already the height of our heads. Scoping for the farmer, I step on the lowest wire and pull the next one up so Jacob can slip through. The metal detector on his back momentarily catches, but he adjusts it quickly before I slip through too. As we begin walking the rows, Jacob slowly scans the dirt with the palm of his machine, and it begins chirping.

The youngest known soldier killed in the First World War was Jacob's age. Jacob, Jim, and Amanda and I actually found his grave in a cemetery so massive I couldn't wrap my head around how many bodies we strode across in our morning wandering there.

On this sunny July afternoon in the farmer's field, my son and I find a number of spent and rusted rifle shells, a handful of shrapnel balls and an unexploded artillery shell that we carefully leave by the driveway of the farmer's home with the knowledge that this is nothing new to him and he will call the proper authorities to have it taken away.

Later that evening, Jacob would disappear, forcing me to call the local police and beg them to help me find my son.

SUMMER 2009 I've been invited by the In Flanders Fields Museum in Ypres to give a speech. It goes well, from what I can tell. I talk about First Nations involvement in the Great War, why so many Canadian Indians volunteered and how good so many of them were at their jobs.

I've got a day off before I fly back home, and so I rent a bicycle. With map in hand, I follow along the moat that surrounds the city, a medieval fortress of sorts that was a hub of commerce in Flanders.

Eventually, I come across the memorial to John McCrae at the site of his field hospital on the edge of the city. I park my bike and wander about, reflect on the poem I still know by heart thirty-five years later. So this was the guy. I stare at a photo of him and shake my head at the tragedy of a man dying of pneumonia and meningitis early in the year that the war would finally end. I also note his similarities to my father. Both of them lieutenant-colonels in the British Expeditionary Force, both highly decorated combat physicians put in charge of hospitals. But my father fought in the Second World War, and he managed, barely, to survive it.

I get back on my bicycle and try to navigate the map that will take me on a fifty-kilometre loop of Flanders Fields, but I get lost as soon as I'm out of the city. What appeared simple isn't so simple at all. I'm looking for sites I wrote about in my first novel: Hill 62, St. Eloi Craters, Kitcheners Wood. I realize how large the killing fields actually were, and certainly how easy it would be for a soldier to become disoriented in what would then have been a featureless hell of mud and barbed wire, dead horses and humans, smashed and splintered forests flattened by massive bombardments, enemies lurking in the stink of it all ready to kill you.

But today, like that day four years before with my son, is beautiful. The poppies swaying in the wind in the ditches and fields are almost a cliché they're so pretty, bright red and larger than I imagined they'd be. I stop and pick a few and press them into a book I'm reading, only to get home a few days later and find that the paper-thin petals have ruptured onto the pages, disintegrating into bloody stains.

I get back on my bike and keep going, wondering for a moment what I'll do if I get a flat tire so far out here in the countryside. I'll be doomed! To be a worrier on a day like today, though, is pointless. And then my thoughts turn to Jacob, to that evening four years ago when he ran away. He had gotten drunk with a group of British teenagers in the big square in Ypres and disappeared with them into the night. When he was eventually returned a day later by the stern yet kind Belgian policemen, Jacob admitted he was only trying to get lucky with a girl he'd fancied. I wanted to ask him if it was worth it, the frantic hours of Amanda and me pacing and phoning and fretting, but then I recognized in his hungover demeanour that there had been no luck at all, that for him the night was an exercise in futility. I remember telling Jacob that boys his age had died in this very place almost a hundred years ago for a cause that was useless too, and how as soon as those words left my mouth I realized the ridiculousness of them. Jacob's angry face only highlighted that what I'd just said wasn't even accidentally funny. Yet still, on this gorgeous day of sun and wind and history, as I bicycle lost through the countryside, I giggle to myself at the memory of that sorry excuse of a rare father–son speech.

But then literal storm clouds appear on the horizon. I'm having a very difficult time picturing—in this landscape of fields and forests undulating all the way to northern France in the distance—what John McCrae and the countless thousands who perished in these fields experienced. For most of my life I've tried to imagine what my father witnessed as he and his troops fought their way through Italy and then the liberation of

Holland. I'd heard a few of the stories: the brutal attrition that was Monte Cassino, how one night my father's advance troops were caught in a German crossfire and he made his way out to them, patching them up and sending them back, one by one, until all that were still alive made it to safety. I especially cherish the story of how, on another night, he got drunk in an *estaminet*, managing to get into a fight with a British general and knocking him out with his valuable doctor's hands. These stories feel so distant, though, like black-and-white photos left out in the sun, starting to fade. The few anecdotes I've heard about McCrae seem even more faded. Despite having tried to imagine living as a soldier of the Great War for many years as I wrote my first novel, I freely admit that so many aspects of that particular experience remain fuzzy to me.

Eventually, I find my way to Hill 62 and park my bike at a café, the idea of a cold Belgian beer sounding really good. I go in to investigate the place and discover that it's also a privately owned museum stuffed with remnants of the Great War, out back a stretch of original British trenches zigzagging through the trees. But what's most amazing is the dozen or so boxes lined up like video poker machines, a stool in front of each one, for viewing 3-D photographs.

I sit at the first and peer into the binocular-like eyepiece of the brown wooden box, and immediately I'm transported nearly one hundred years back to the madness of the war. I feel like I'm watching the scene from a window, the image is so real: French soldiers march past a dead horse, the men shockingly alive, the face of each one of them exhausted, mud sticking to their boots as they trudge past the horse, its tongue lolling out. The men step by it as if they don't even see it.

The backlit photo is stunning in its detail, and when I turn a knob, another appears, this one of a dead German soldier propped up against a trench, his deteriorating face grinning, the distinctive helmet still strapped to his head, his clothes in tatters, his legs crossed as if he's resting and waiting for something. I turn the knob again, and here's another, a British biplane crashed in a field, its unlucky pilot hanging mangled out of his cockpit. And another, this one of a sniper's nest constructed in the trunk of a splintered tree. If I look closely enough, I can see the barrel of the sniper's rifle pointing at me.

I make my way from machine to machine, dozens and dozens of photos in each. And as the late morning turns to early afternoon, I realize that, in these incredible images, the world I'd tried so hard to bring to life finally truly comes to life in front of my eyes. And I realize the irony: sitting here in a musty room in an old house in Belgium, I am witnessing the world around me unfold in a far more real way than the actual world outside ever could. I am sitting in this musty room in Belgium, moving from machine to machine, moving from stool to stool, speed dating with the dead, the horror of a past I finally get to see in a dimension I've not ever been able to imagine before.

I see my father, finally. I see John McCrae. I begin to see some of the scenes that those two men must have similarly seen, this utter brutality forced upon all of nature, created by man. I finally see; it's through the eyes of the people that haunt these photos, these ghosts who materialize in a world I'd only until now flatly envisioned. Wishing Jacob could be here to see these images with me, I make the decision to spend the afternoon with the photos inside this dark place rather than bicycle in the sunshine of the Ypres Salient, because here in this room the world has opened up.

SUMMER 2015 I've been invited back by the city of Ypres this coming June to spend a month reflecting on the centennial of the Great War and sharing my thoughts with the public. I write this now in the early spring of 2015 in the hope that the summer approaching might in part be spent this way:

Jacob, my son, will come with me. He'll be twenty-five then, and so if he runs away, I won't worry so much about him.

My friend Jim Steel, he'll come. He's only just recently lost his wife, the love of his life, Maria, and so maybe this trip will allow him to wander, if only briefly, away from his world of private grief as we explore this landscape impossible to come to terms with: a place at once so beautiful and yet really just one vast cemetery a metal detector's beep below the surface.

Amanda, my wife, will join us too. This time, she won't be so stressed out by my son's behaviour that her hair begins to fall out. Instead, she might even climb on a bicycle and pedal with us through the place that has obsessed her husband for a long, long time, enjoying the sun and the wind rippling the fields, and feeling the anchor, the weight of what lies just beneath us. Amanda is someone who deeply understands what exists beyond the world we can see.

And I will wander with these three special people, remembering the night my son ran away so long ago, and I will remember the morning I was eight and woke up to find that my father had died, and I will recall the day I pedalled quite accidentally up to John McCrae's memorial and later witnessed the "Last Post" at Menin Gate, and how these confluences, for the briefest of moments, all made sense to me. And I want to believe I will finally come to terms somehow with the idea that life is, in some small part, this: you will see someone you love one moment and then the next the horror will sink in that you will never see that person again.

But most importantly, it's this: we are here now. Yes, we are here now in part to remember and to honour the past. But we are here now. We breathe. And we've been given the chance to live with those who live alongside us, to share in their despair and celebrate their happy moments. I want to go back to Ypres this summer to experience this simple truth most of all.

Detail of the central bronze sculpture decorating the National War Memorial, Ottawa. Designed by Vernon March and dedicated by King George V in 1939, the sculpture features twenty-two figures (including two women), representing each branch of the Canadian forces that served in World War I.

GEORGE ELLIOTT CLARKE
FROM THE DIARY OF
WILLIAM ANDREW WHITE
á Lajoux, Jura, France, Décembre 1917

I.

A powerful rain
dins down these mountains,
rinses peak snow into hellish streams,
floods gully and pitfall.
Graves yawn open now everywhere.

(Some Christmas . . .
A *Somme* Christmas . . .

I'm down to the last crumb of cake—
and no wine—
never wine.)

We dark men are sent to—
are meant to—
stand under this inundation,

The son of former slaves, Reverend Captain William Andrew White was
George Elliott Clarke's great-grandfather and a Nova Scotian who became
the first black officer in the British Army, serving as a chaplain.

this dark, hard-driving wet,
and labour hard, axing
logs, laboriously,
our drenching making harder the work,
but also making slippery the axes,
so that it's harder to make a dent
in the liquefying woods,

and easier to make a dent in your own legs—
or a friend's—
or in a friend's lagging head.

II.

Aye, we're at loggerheads
with dunderheads—
our Christian brethren Canucks,
here in France, but nigh Geneva—

the Xmas crèches and chocolates—
in the milk-topped, neutral,
unconquerable, Swiss Alps.

We're here because of a battering ram
of Right
that let us butt our way
into the White Man's War—
belligerent clans and bellicose states—
to feel the privilege of perishing
to preserve George V,

but also so we can see ourselves stand tall
in our sons' eyes.

I'm here so that Coloured Christian Canucks
are not destitute of a down-home preacher.

I serve the King Eternal—
His fiery Crown,
His blazing Cross.

I have relinquished Domesticity
to live fully at ordered Liberty,
advancing my Ministry,

to even minister to wounds
and ills—

gashes and pleurisy,
pneumonia and tuberculosis—

what kill us—

Canadian Forestry Corps infantry—
the No. 2 Construction troop—

far from the Huns' bullets,
barbed-wire, and bayonets.

III.

But our poor lungs are spent
in the duty to lop forests—
to splinter wood for rail ties—
so porridge-faced poilu can choo-choo to the Front
and take potshots at the Krauts

after beer and bacon,
tea and tobacco,
wine and whores.

Irony: We serve where Hannibal romped
and ramped elephants upon Rome—
and where Dictator Napoléon
tamped down Haiti's rebellious L'Ouverture . . .
But glacial *History* freezes us out.

IV.

The Western Front is due north
of us,
so the bad news trickles south.

I hear it's a mishmash of *Conjectures*—
bad plans, bad commands—

hollers in dirty horse French
or hoarse, bitter Cockney—

so, in a day, thousands prove
incarnately incarnadine—

bomb-blast-earthquake-overthrown,

toppled into mud pits—
curious tombs—

to be gnawed open by rats' teeth.

Utmost scarlet brims each trench.

Still holding half a brow,
half a jaw,
one eye,
an abortive helmet sprawls,

but is multiplied thousandly.

Or one sees gas-poisoned saints stagger,
with bandages for eyes.

Or the half-dead stroll like Zombies,
eyes fixed on a fixed horizon,
heedless of gun flash,
likely shot-deafened,
either courageous fools,
or displaying nerves never sham.

Still, angry grey storms of lead
scatter headless massacres

in Antichrist's charnel-house church—

the ruddy meal of the battlefield—

the doubly bloody,
narcotic feast,
fit for maggots, *racaille*.

I've heard that shells thud the earth so hard,
corpses jiggle with the shock,

and skeletons protrude suddenly
where earthy fires jet smoke—

and flames limp, sprint, hop, skip—

in a darkling sky;

or the spectral *merde* of chlorine harries,
worries,
those alive enough to breathe and fall,
wriggling in mire,
facing Death's temporary *Cataclysm*.

All about rampage Vickers guns,
and nervous horses stamping every inch of turf
with pulsing blood,

while blasts and detonations
boom and boom and boom . . .

V.

Imported—as if conquerors—to France,
we black men decamped to this war
with drums barking, bagpipes bawling,

first disciplined
by threats of lynching and frets of Klan,

only to discover our old-new discipline is *Labour*—
unreneged Negro *Slavery*—
to roustabout in woods
and muscle down trees,
our sweat raining.

Until light-bodied mosquitoes
bear us lightly away.

Verily, it's *Disease* that slaughters us:

A brother goes rabid with sweat;
his face springs curving tears;
he lisps prayers and spiels curses;
then succumbs, in fits,
after a rattling whisper.

With mine own tears,
I try to warm his cold, drying bloodstream—
his chilling body—
the wax treasure that's now his corpse.

(It's good that,
even between soldiers,
Tenderness is legal.)

As the African chaplain,
as the single Coloured Officer (thus far)
among the male millions
the British Army fields,

it is my task to prepare us black men

to be Christian soldiers,

and deliver *Death* to the Kaiser's kin
and die, kinless, ourselves,

if so's our *Fate*.

VI.

Today's sky is a vault of water—
and the earth is unfathomable mud;

our dark shadows, flashing axes,
slash the rain.

When it ends, we see the mountains breathe
white clouds and snow,

and as the sun sets like the lit end
of a cigarette,

clouds lap up its light
with grey finality.

Still, I've enough left to write
this inky candle-light,

then to ignite the candle
that lit up Christ,

illuminating the Apostles' quill pens.

Now, we see through a glass, darkly,

until *Death* smashes that blood-stained window
hiding Heaven from us.

[Kelowna (British Columbia) 30 Septembre–2 Octobre MMXIV]

HANNAH MOSCOVITCH
WRITING ABOUT WAR

> Why am I interested in recon marines in an unpopular war?
> Why am I interested in musicians in a dystopian and
> damaged city? Why am I interested in this?
>
> DAVID SIMON,
> creator of *The Wire*, *Generation Kill* and *Treme*

I SPENT A LOT of my middle school and teenage years reading about the Holocaust. I was a lonely kid, and my Auschwitz books probably didn't help me make friends, plus the reading led to a series of dreams set in gas chambers, and it made me feel alienated from the affluent middle-class society I lived in: Ottawa in the 1990s. But I got stuck on it, for reasons that haven't been all that clear to me. I think I felt a sort of personal horror because I'm half Jewish, but lots of Jewish kids don't spend their free time reading *The Rise and Fall of the Third Reich*.

Some kids are very into sharks. I was into the Holocaust.

IN 2007, when Canadian troops were seeing active combat in Panjwaii and Arghandab, I started writing about the war in Afghanistan. I got a call from one of the creators of *Afghanada*, a hit CBC Radio drama that offered a grunt's eye view of the war.

Maurice Cullen, "Dead Horse and Rider in a Trench" (detail), 1918.

My reason for wanting to write on the show had nothing to do with the conflict itself. I liked the show—I liked its characters—but mostly my ego was involved, heavily involved, because all of the other writers on the show had good careers, and I wanted to become more like them and less like myself.

The thing is, I started to get stuck on the war in Afghanistan the way I had been stuck on the Holocaust. At first, I was amazingly ignorant about it and about military protocol and culture in general. But I quickly became familiar with the various war journalists and correspondents reporting from Afghanistan. I read their articles and books and absorbed their insights. If you're ripping stories from the headlines, you feel some responsibility to convey news, to be rigorous, to be methodical, and it was my intense researching for the show that jump-started my obsession with the war.

We worked with military consultants on Afghanada who were hired by the show to read scripts, answer our questions and generally help us with authenticity. Our consultants were soldiers who had done tours in Panjwaii and Arghandab and were now home from the war. I started off asking questions like "What is an IED?" or "What is a medevac?" And they would smile and say, "an improvised explosive device," or "the chopper that takes you to the hospital at KAF if you're hit." The subtext was "Are you stupid?" Four years later, my questions sounded more like this: "Would the Apache chain guns be in range for that?"

In the middle of all of this, I was up late on a Saturday night researching online, and I watched a clip of a Taliban beheading. The video made me sick, mostly because it was so much worse than what I'd imagined. I thought I would see a blindfolded man kneeling and then there'd be a single clean blow of a sword to his neck. Instead, the man being executed was hog-tied and held down on the ground. Next, there was a lot of slow sawing back and forth with what looked like a blunt knife, and the man was writhing, and there was a sluice of black liquid that came out of his throat. I got up and walked around my apartment for a few minutes. Then I went and stood over the sink in the bathroom, let saliva drip out of my mouth. I started to wonder why I was doing this with my Saturday nights.

But I was too obsessed to stop. I submitted a proposal to the Banff Centre to write a play about Canadian forces in Panjwaii, and I received a commission and a residency from them. I started to show pieces of my new writing to close friends, who were mostly confused. They didn't get what the fascination was. Military culture grossed them out, and the war didn't interest them. It was just another horrific international conflict that they read about online. On top of that, a lot of them had no idea we were at war: they thought that what we were doing in Afghanistan was called "war" for official reasons but that it was actually more like peacekeeping. For them, reckoning with my project meant acknowledging Canada's shifting international role.

When I finally premiered my play about Afghanistan, titled *This Is War*, Canadian audiences had a similarly stunned reaction. They were dead silent throughout the performance. Afterwards, they expressed a lot of shock and incomprehension. They didn't like what I was showing them, and they would tell me they were sorry they'd seen it. The play was later produced in Chicago, and I noticed that Americans were less put off by it: they knew they were at war and had a clearer understanding of what that meant. It was a strange relief to spend time in a more hawkish culture, where my fixation was less distasteful.

The weird thing was, I could see it, in little flashes, from the

Canadian point of view. The war in Afghanistan involved a tiny fraction of our population. Like my close friends, the theatre-going crowd hadn't voted for the government that was expanding and prolonging our operations in Afghanistan. They didn't want to know about it. Meanwhile, I was obsessing over photos of our soldiers on tour in Afghanistan, men covered in tats that read "infidel" who between firefights were punching each other out of boredom and pinning up raunchy porn. It seemed an unlikely fascination, even to me.

A TRUISM ABOUT GUERRILLA STYLE, asymmetrical warfare is that the invading army has better equipment but the invaded people are more familiar with the terrain. The Hamid Karzai government might have invited NATO into Afghanistan, but the Taliban viewed the coalition forces as an occupying power and they vehemently counterattacked. The Taliban were outnumbered and outgunned, but they riddled the countryside with IEDs. If you were a Canadian soldier walking around in Panjwaii, you were in constant danger of having your legs blown off and, depending on the size and angle of the bomb, also your genitals. Another truism of guerrilla warfare is that the enemy is not identifiable. There was nothing to distinguish a Taliban combatant from a civilian. Lots of farmers in Afghan-istan carry weapons. So if a fighting-age man approaches you holding a Kalashnikov, what do you do? Do you fire on him before he fires on you? Or do you wait to see if he is a Taliban fighter? Do you wait for him to try to kill you before you engage? In Afghanistan, suicide bombers were often young boys who were, say, riding a bicycle towards you. So what do you do? Do you shoot a fourteen-year-old? If you do shoot him, you've shot a child. If you don't shoot him, you could be killed, along with all the guys standing near you. The uncertainty—uncertainty on the level of "Will I get my balls blown off today?"—led to a lot of fear on the part of the soldiers. It also led to a lot of crushingly difficult ethical decision-making. Soldiers, operating in unknown terrain and rightly paranoid about being fired on or blown up, were forced to make impossible choices.

I had carte blanche with the military consultants on *Afghanada* to pose invasive questions, so I asked a soldier working with us (one who I was pretty sure had seen a lot of active combat) what it was like to be in these paralyzing situations. He said, "You make the call you think you can live with." Later, when we'd both had a lot to drink, he said to me, "The worst thing is killing a child. It's hard to come back from that. Those guys are fucked."

In "In Flanders Fields," Lieutenant-Colonel John McCrae invoked the dead to remind soldiers of their duty: with "failing hands" the dying pass the torch of war to those still living. In the spirit of McCrae's famous poem, many soldiers who fought in the war in Afghanistan tattooed the names of fallen friends on their arms to remind them of what they were fighting for. But modern psychiatry has revealed that accountability to the dead has a dark side.

Hanging out with soldiers, I started to catch undercurrents of tension. I'd notice that one of our military consultants couldn't stop giggling—an unlikely high-pitched sound—when he told us about firing on the Taliban. Or I'd become aware of an inability to meet my eye, combined with a volatile cheerfulness. And then there were the more obvious indicators: an offhand joke about not being able to sleep without a night light on, or vomiting after eating meat, or punching a hole in a wall. And finally, there were the glaringly blatant cases, like the slow withdrawal of one military consultant into an alcoholic stupor. I'd call him for notes and he'd be drinking beers in his truck while driving one-handed down dark rural roadways. I started to get the sense that this behaviour was the after-effect of those split-second decisions, and that all the competing ethical pressures on the psyche of the soldiers were being made visible.

Military psychologists later explained post-traumatic stress disorder to me: that there is huge trauma associated with witnessing or being the victim of a horrific event (or a series of horrific events, which is what war is). Returning Canadian soldiers who had not only witnessed but also been the agent of one of these events suffer from a darker form of PTSD. Soldiers who fired on people who might have been civilians or turned out not to be suicide bombers were traumatized by their actions. They became their own victims. These soldiers, the military psychiatrists told me, were often the hardest to help, because their guilt overrode all attempts to rehabilitate them. They had been making the calls they thought they could live with but then finding out later that they couldn't live with them at all.

It sheds light on human nature to talk to people who have had to make the most difficult choices possible: moral dilemmas so extreme that they injure the brain. We know that war exposes and shifts character (which is why boys, traditionally, went to war to "become men" or to "find out what kind of men they were"). War shows us what happens when humans come up against extremes. And here's what I think happens: Our own extremes are exposed. Our altruism and psychopathy are laid bare. If you're interested in human psychology, like I am, war is a shortcut to the answers. I've learned from war that the human psyche is bizarrely flexible and complex, that a person is capable both of immense, intelligent selflessness and banal evil, that a single human action can contain heroism and brutality, or callousness and tenderness, that there is nothing simple to say about us. Once you think you've got hold of some truth about humans, war will show you the opposite, and beyond that, something more complex than the opposite. Studying humans in war will strip you of all your certainty, all your theses, all your analysis, and leave you trying to say something about our nature in mediums that suggest rather than denote: poetry, fiction, drama.

AFTER A PERFORMANCE of This Is War in Chicago, I did a talkback with the audience. A young guy in a Blackhawks sweatshirt asked me a question about the injuries sustained by one of the characters in the play. He wanted to know, "Can that really happen to your balls?" I smiled a little, because of course the young guy in the Blackhawks sweatshirt was asking me that. I said, "Yes." The Taliban pack shards of metal—nails, metal filings—into their IEDs in order to inflict the most damage. And because military medicine is so good these days, you can survive multiple severe injuries, or polytraumas as they're called. Men who've been blinded and had both legs amputated and lost their genitals do survive.

The young man thanked me for my answer.

At the end of the session, he came up to me. He was holding his girlfriend by the hand. He looked nineteen, maybe twenty, years old. He was very soft-spoken. He said, "I just found out I'm being deployed to Panjwaii in two weeks. I didn't know about that kind of injury. I hope it doesn't happen to me."

And then we stood there—him and his girlfriend and me—and we all looked at each other for a long time.

I felt a lot of things: stupid, and curious about him, and scared for him, and weirdly close to him because he'd said something vulnerable. I didn't know how to get the mix of things I was thinking into words.

Muddied and bloodied: Manitoba sappers (tunnel diggers) just back from
Vimy Ridge, France, January 1917.

ABOUT THE CONTRIBUTORS

Lieutenant-General (Ret'd) ROMÉO DALLAIRE served
thirty-five years with the Canadian Armed Forces and eight years
in the Canadian Senate. His Governor General's Award–winning
book, *Shake Hands with the Devil*, exposed the failures of the
international community to stop the Rwandan genocide.
His second book, *They Fight Like Soldiers, They Die Like Children*,
describes the Child Soldier phenomenon and offers solutions to
eradicate it: a mission to which Dallaire has committed the rest of
his life. He is also a respected advocate for the prevention of
genocide and mass atrocities, as well as an outspoken champion
of veterans, particularly those who suffer from PTSD. He is the
recipient of many honours and awards, including the Order of
Canada and the Pearson Peace Medal.

TIM COOK is the Great War historian at the Canadian War
Museum, as well as an adjunct professor at Carleton University.
His books have won numerous awards, including the 2008 J.W.
Dafoe Prize for *At the Sharp End* and the 2009 Charles Taylor Prize
for Literary Non-Fiction for *Shock Troops*. In 2013, he received the
Pierre Berton Award for popularizing Canadian history, and in
2014 he was appointed a member of the Order of Canada. Cook
lives in Ottawa with his family.

Poppy display outside the Menin Gate, Ypres, Belgium.

PATRICK LANE has received numerous awards for his writing, including the Governor General's Award for Poetry and the Canadian Authors Association Award. Among his books is the memoir *There Is a Season*, which won the Lieutenant Governor's Award for Literary Excellence and the inaugural British Columbia Award for Canadian Non-fiction, and a critically acclaimed novel, *Red Dog, Red Dog*. Lane is a member of the Order of Canada and lives near Victoria, B.C.

MARY JANIGAN is a journalist who has written extensively about Canadian public policy, including politics and economics, for the *Toronto Star*, *Maclean's* and the *Globe and Mail*. She has won the prestigious Hy Solomon Award for policy analysis, and the National Newspaper Award for her clause-by-clause scrutiny of proposed Constitution changes. Her book about the Canadian "West versus the Rest," *Let the Eastern Bastards Freeze in the Dark*, was a national bestseller and winner of the J. W. Dafoe Book Prize. She lives in Toronto, but travels as much as she can, at the flicker of a passport.

KEN DRYDEN was first elected to the House of Commons in 2004 and served as a member of Parliament for seven years. He is well-known for his achievements as a goaltender for the Montreal Canadiens hockey team from 1971 to 1979, during which time the team won six Stanley Cups. In 1984, he was appointed Ontario's first youth commissioner. He is the author of five bestselling books: *The Game*, *Home Game*, *The Moved and the Shaken*, *In School*, and *Becoming Canada*. Ken and his wife, Lynda, have two grown children and four grandchildren.

KEVIN PATTERSON grew up in Selkirk, Manitoba, and put himself through medical school by enlisting in the Canadian Army. He began to write while stationed at Camp Shilo, outside Brandon, Manitoba, and studied creative writing at UBC. His critically acclaimed books include a memoir titled *The Water in Between*, a *Globe and Mail* best book and an international bestseller; a short story collection, *Country of Cold*, winner of the Rogers Writers' Trust Fiction Prize; a novel, *Consumption*; and *Outside the Wire*, a collection of first-hand accounts from the front lines of Canada's war in Afghanistan (edited with Jane Warren). He lives on Saltspring Island, B.C.

MARGARET ATWOOD, whose work has been published in thirty-five countries, is the author of more than forty books of fiction, poetry and critical essays. Her novels include *Cat's Eye*, short-listed for the 1989 Booker Prize; *Alias Grace*, which won the Giller Prize in Canada and the Premio Mondello in Italy; *The Blind Assassin*, winner of the 2000 Booker Prize; *Oryx and Crake*, short-listed for the 2003 Man Booker Prize; *The Year of the Flood*; *MaddAddam*; and her most recent, *The Heart Goes Last*. She is the recipient of the Los Angeles Times Innovator's Award, and lives in Toronto with the writer Graeme Gibson.

WADE DAVIS is the bestselling author of several books, including *The Serpent and the Rainbow*, *One River* and, most recently, *Into the Silence*, winner of the Samuel Johnson Prize. He is an award-winning anthropologist, ethnobotanist, filmmaker and photographer. Between 1999 and 2013 he served as Explorer-in-Residence at the National Geographic Society and is currently a member of the NGS Explorers Council. Davis is a professor of anthropology and the B.C. Leadership Chair in Cultures and Ecosystems at Risk at the University of British Columbia.

FRANCES ITANI is the author of sixteen books including the #1 bestselling WWI novel *Deafening*, winner of a Commonwealth Writers' Prize for Best Book and finalist for the International IMPAC Dublin Literary Award; and a follow-up novel, *Tell*, which was shortlisted for the Scotiabank Giller Prize. Her short stories have won two Ottawa Book Awards for fiction, and she is a three-time winner of the CBC Literary Award. A member of the Order of Canada, Itani practised and taught nursing before beginning to write. She lives in Ottawa.

JONATHAN VANCE holds the J.B. Smallman Chair in the department of history at the University of Western Ontario, where he teaches military history, Canadian history and social memory. He is the author of many books, including *Death So Noble: Memory, Meaning, and the First World War*, winner of the 1997 J.W. Dafoe Book Prize; and *A History of Canadian Culture*, winner of the 2009 Lela Common Award from the Canadian Authors Association.

JOSEPH BOYDEN's first novel, *Three Day Road*, won numerous awards including the Rogers Writers' Trust Fiction Prize. His second novel, *Through Black Spruce*, was awarded the Scotiabank Giller Prize and his third novel, *The Orenda*, was the 2014 winner of Canada Reads. In 2012, Boyden received the Queen Elizabeth II Diamond Jubilee Medal for his contributions to Canadian art and culture. Boyden is a member of the creative writing faculty at the University of British Columbia in Vancouver, Canada, and at the Institute of American Indian Arts in Santa Fe, New Mexico. He divides his time between Northern Ontario and Louisiana.

GEORGE ELLIOTT CLARKE is the poet laureate of Toronto and a librettist, novelist, playwright, screenwriter, and scholar. He won the Governor General's Award for Poetry in 2001 for *Execution Poems*; since then he has received the Martin Luther King Jr. Achievement Award and the Pierre Elliott Trudeau Fellowship Prize. His first novel, *George and Rue*, was published in 2005, and his next novel, *The Motorcyclist*, will be published in 2016. Clarke was the William Lyon Mackenzie King Visiting Professor in Canadian Studies at Harvard University in 2013–14, and is currently the E.J. Pratt Professor of Canadian Literature at the University of Toronto.

HANNAH MOSCOVITCH is one of Canada's most produced playwrights. Her work has won multiple Dora Mavor Moore awards and she has been nominated for the Governor General's Award, the Carol Bolt Award, the Toronto Arts Council Foundation Emerging Artist Award, the K.M. Hunter Award, the Siminovitch Prize and the international Susan Smith Blackburn Prize. She was a contributing writer for the CBC drama series *Afghanada* from 2007 to 2011, and her recent play *This Is War* won the Trillium Book Award and the Toronto Critic's Award for Best Canadian Play.

CONTRIBUTORS' CREDITS

IMAGE CREDITS

Endpaper (*front*): David Milne, "Courcelette from the Cemetery, 26 July 1919", National Gallery of Canada

Page i: Library and Archives Canada, PA-002165

Page ii: Ann Taylor-Hughes/Getty Images

Page iii: Library and Archives Canada, PA-008040

Page iv: Blake Heathcote/Testaments of Honour

Page v: Alex Linghorn/Getty Images

Page vi: Courtesy of Guelph Museums, McCrae House

Page x: Blake Heathcote/Testaments of Honour

Page xi: Library and Archives Canada, PA-002482

Pages xii–xiii: Erlend Robaye/Erroba/Getty Images

Page xiv: City of Toronto Archives, Fonds 1244, Item 727

Page 5: Godong/Getty Images

Page 10: Library and Archives Canada, PA-001513

Page 15: Courtesy of Toronto Public Library

Page 16: Courtesy of Guelph Museums, McCrae House

Page 21: Courtesy of Guelph Museums, McCrae House

Page 26: Courtesy of Guelph Museums, McCrae House

Page 31: Courtesy of Guelph Museums, McCrae House

Page 44: Library and Archives Canada, PA-000544

Pages 52–53: Courtesy of Guelph Museums, McCrae House

Pages 56–57: Library and Archives Canada, C-104799

Page 58: City of Toronto Archives, Fonds 200, Series 372, Subseries 1

Page 73: Helen Main/Getty Images

Page 74: Library and Archives Canada, ACC. NO. 1983–28–738

Page 86–87: "If Ye Break Faith" Victory Bonds Poster, CWM 19850475-013, Canadian War Museum

Page 96: Montreal *Gazette* photo archives

Page 102: City of Toronto Archives, Fonds 1244, Item 829

Page 103: Blake Heathcote/Testaments of Honour

Page 104: Library and Archives Canada, PA-001479

Page 105: Library and Archives Canada, PA-001805

Page 106: Courtesy of the Imperial War Museum, Q04556

Page 107: Library and Archives Canada, PA-001464

Pages 108–109: Library and Archives Canada, PA-001921

Page 110: (top) Library and Archives Canada, PA-000581;
           (bottom) Library and Archives Canada, PA-001693

Page 111: Library and Archives Canada, PA-003419

Page 112: Library and Archives Canada, PA-001679

Pages 118–119: Library and Archives Canada, PA-002864

Page 124: Archives of Ontario, 10028224

Pages 132–133: William Vanderson/Getty Images

Page 134: Bob Davis Photography/Getty Images

Page 140: Public Archives of Newfoundland and Labrador,
           The Rooms Provincial Archives, VA 36–38.2

Pages 144–145: Knopf Canada

Page: 152: Courtesy of the Imperial War Museum, Q02041

Page 153: Courtesy of Guelph Museums, McCrae House

Page 170: Library and Archives Canada, C-014590

Page 176: Courtesy of Frances Itani

Page 181: Nige Burton/Getty Images

Pages 186–187: A.Y. Jackson, "A Copse, Evening",
           CWM 19710261-0186, Beaverbrook Collection of War Art,
           Canadian War Museum

Page 188: Public domain

Pages 194, 201: Ley and Lois Smith War, Memory and Popular Research
           Collection/The University of Western Ontario/London,
           Ontario

Page 206: Library and Archives Canada, PA-003011

Page 207: Library and Archives Canada, PA-000787

Page 208: *(top left)* Library and Archives Canada, PA-003759;
(top right) Library and Archives Canada, PA-003763;
(bottom left) Library and Archives Canada, PA-003765;
(bottom right) Public Archives of Newfoundland and Labrador,
The Rooms Provincial Archives, VA 157–54

Page 209: Library and Archives Canada, PA-002211

Page 210: Library and Archives Canada, PA-002857

Page 211: Library and Archives Canada, PA-003392

Pages 212–213: *(top)* Library and Archives Canada, PA-002281;
(bottom) Library and Archives Canada, PA-002562

Page 214: Public Archives of Newfoundland and Labrador,
The Rooms Provincial Archives, PANL NA-3106

Page 215: Blake Heathcote/Testaments of Honour

Page 216: Library and Archives Canada, PA-001581

Page 225: Images Etc Ltd/Getty Images

Page 226: Knopf Canada

Page 236: Maurice Cullen, "Dead Horse and Rider in a Trench",
CWM 19710261–0126, Beaverbrook Collection of War Art,
Canadian War Museum

Page 245: Courtesy of Archives of Manitoba, N20962

Page 246: Godong/Getty Images

Page 252: bob/Getty Images

Endpaper *(facing page 252)*: Courtesy of Guelph Museums,
McCrae House

Endpaper *(back)*: Gail Shortlander/Getty Images

Case *(front and back)*: CS Richardson

IN FLANDERS FIELDS: 100 YEARS

Conceived and edited by: Amanda Betts
Managing editor: Deirdre Molina
Archival image research: Blake Heathcote
Copy editor: Alex Schultz
Design: CS Richardson
Production: Brittany Larkin

Typeset in Quadraat and Neutraface

Opposite: John McCrae's original grave marker, Wimereaux, France.